CW00557146

THE SPECIALIST GUNDOG

TRAINING THE RIGHT BREED FOR SHOOTING WILD GAME

BY THE SAME AUTHOR

The Versatile Gundog

THE SPECIALIST GUNDOG

Training the Right Breed for Shooting Wild Game

GUY WALLACE

Foreword by
KEITH ERLANDSON

THE SPORTSMAN'S PRESS
LONDON

Published by The Sportsman's Press 2002

For Heather and Jack
Hoping that they may be lucky enough to take part in some of the sport that I have enjoyed

A catalogue record for this book is available from the British Library

ISBN 0-948253-82-7

Printed in Great Britain by The Bath Press Limited

Contents

List of Plates

Foreword
by Keith Erlandson

According to the great Irish authority, John Nash, whose name frequently appears in *The Specialist Gundog*, the first written works on those dogs which today we would classify as gundogs, emanated from the pens of Spanish and Italian masters circa the fourteenth century. Nash in fact claims he taught himself Italian in order that he could peruse such ancient tomes but oddly enough, William Arkwright, author of the classic *The Pointer and His Predecessors*, made the same claim, so was Nash indulging in a little Celtic fantasy?

It would appear that the first mention of the ancestors of our present day gundogs appeared in *The Mayster of Game* by Edward, Duke of York, who fell at the battle of Agincourt in 1415 . It was followed in 1486 by a treatise on hunting and falconry, *The Boke of St. Albans* by Dame Juliana Berners, who made some reference to 'Spaynels'.

Arguably the first author to write a book in the English language on gundogs which were expected to perform a function as shooting dogs, more or less as they do today, was General Hutchinson with his *Dog Breaking*, first published in 1848. Several works followed Hutchinson's book, which arguably set the tone for less violent training and handling of dogs for the shooting field but the total volume of such works is far smaller than the number of books written around other fields of human activity, such as ball games, motor cars and motor racing, sailing, golf and gardening.

Nevertheless, I personally believed that the subject of gundog training had been well covered by what had been already published from Hutchinson onwards and anything further in this sphere would be surplus to requirements. The last books I had seen on gundog training I would describe, as reading material, like wading through treacle in fisherman's chest waders.

The title of this book, *The Specialist Gundog*, confused me somewhat as this seemed to imply that the book would cover only one specialist breed of gundog, or at the most a specific group, like spaniels, retrievers, bird dogs or continentals but the book does in fact break the mould completely regarding anything that has ever been written before upon the subject, in as much as it covers every breed of dog within these shores, with a description of its characteristics and what its function(s) is/are.

In view of what is already available regarding gundog literature, to fill a need which is not already catered for, any new book would have to be different from anything else already available. This book is, as no book has ever been written before which covers the selection, care, training and working function of every group: retrievers, spaniels, native pointers and setters and the hunt, point and retrieve breeds from the Continent. In addition, there is much valuable information on the training and use of deer dogs for woodland stalking, a topical addition as woodland deerstalking is gaining momentum. As an extra, it covers dogs working with hawks and long-winged falcons, and falconry is another growth sport which the author took part in when there were only about 40 falconers in the country, against 4,000 today.

A most refreshing aspect of this book is that although field trials are mentioned in passing, the author has never indulged in field trial competitions and has developed a far healthier attitude to gundog work than would be possible for the average trialler, to whom winning is so important and who seldom can avoid being dragged into the sometimes incestuous politics of the game. I have always maintained that politics do not help a dog to hunt harder or find its game better and this is reflected in the relaxed attitude of the author to all aspects of gundog work.

Preface

I count myself extremely fortunate. Not only have I been lucky enough to spend my life following and actually hunting different packs of hounds, working many excellent (and not so excellent) ferrets, terriers and running dogs, stalking hill and woodland deer and flying both hawks and falcons all over the world but I have also been privileged to regularly shoot just about every British game species except ptarmigan. If I fished I should do even less work than I do already! While practising these sports I have been eternally grateful for the excellent company of my fellow sportsmen and women from all walks of life (soon, it would appear, to be outlawed at perverted criminals), many of whom have deserved the ultimate accolade of being called one of Nature's Gentlemen and most of whom were educated at 'The Rural University'. (One has also had to suffer the inevitable rogues and fools.) It has also been a privilege to follow one's sport in the breathtaking scenery for which country sports are largely responsible. However, my greatest enjoyment has come from those splendid working dogs without which none of these wonderful sports would have been possible. Time and again they have given their all and they have always been honest and genuine characters with no 'side' to them at all.

For the last 20-plus years I have been training gundogs professionally for rough and driven shooting, deerstalking and falconry. It would appear, though, that virtually all the numerous gundog training books available assume that one is going to go rough shooting for predominantly rabbits and pheasants with an English springer spaniel or shoot driven pheasants over a labrador. However, I know countless sportsmen who would sooner shoot pigeons over decoys or coming in to roost than any 200-bird pheasant day or to whom the lure of the foreshore in a freezing January dawn or the rolling heather clad hills in August far outweighs that of the covertside. They frequently ask me about training gundogs for their particular sport and it is for those fellow sportsmen that this book is written. There is also a welcome return to the basic 'hunting' of wild game in the continental sense of the word by many who have had enough of large bags of driven pheasants 'to order'. One of the great attractions of the wild quarry mentioned in this book is the 'Glorious Uncertainty' of Here Today and Gone Tomorrow. Nothing can be taken for granted and every shot is a bonus.

I trained my first springer shortly after leaving school, with the late Peter Moxon's excellent book *Gundogs: Training and Field Trials* (10s 6d) in one hand and the dog on a leather lead in the other and we both eventually got there. Thereafter I fear, apart from a book on training pointers in America and some books for review, have never read another one! However, I have been fortunate in having the two greatest tutors in the world at my disposal – the game and the dogs themselves. I trust that I have had the wit to learn from them.

I had better state here and now that I do not have a favourite breed of gundog. I have never suffered from 'chronic springeritis' or 'terminal labradoritis'. I invariably both own myself and train for clients retrievers, spaniels, 'English' pointers and setters and Hunter Pointer Retrievers (HPRs) for a variety of different jobs. (I have a photo of no less than eleven different gundog breeds here for training.) Indeed, recently a small group of us were walking up grouse in what was once Radnorshire and it took a fellow gun to point out that I had a labrador walking at heel, a springer questing immediately to my front while an 'English' pointer and a weimaraner were alternately quartering from flank to flank. To me it was merely four young dogs learning their trade. There is no perfect breed. Some dogs within a litter, let alone within a breed, are better at some jobs than others. Our parents doubtless hoped that we would all be Olympic-class athletes with a Double First at 'Oxbridge' – most of them have been sadly disappointed! However, certain breeds of gundog have been selectively bred for generations to do specific jobs and it makes sense to choose a breed developed to suit your *main* type of sport. However. I take the view that a person will always get on better with a breed that they like and want despite its inherent shortcomings rather than a breed thrust down their throat by a so-called expert. I know of a man who stalks successfully over a Pekinese and I recently saw a Great Dane picking up on a grouse moor but I could not seriously recommend either! There are also many breeds of dog other than gundogs that are equally suitable for particular shooting sports, i.e. terriers and lurchers for rabbiting or Alsatians (GSDs) and Bavarian Mountain Bloodhounds for woodland deerstalking. I shall also refer to them where appropriate. There are also many cross breeds of two working breeds that are also eminently suitable. It is really a question of 'horses for courses'.

As a professional I make no apology for regarding a gundog purely as a tool with which to do a job of work although I accept that the average gundog is a family pet for 365 days in the year and a working dog on possibly only 10, 20 or 30 of them. That is fine as long as one remembers that it is a dog and it expects to be treated like a dog.

The ability to train a dog is not one of those mystical gifts bestowed by The Almighty upon a chosen few. Anyone with half-an-hour a day, a little of that rare commodity called common sense and, above all, the commitment can turn out a working dog that is a credit to the trainer and a joy to take out in the field. However it is as well to be clear how and what one is trying to teach the dog before starting out because if the trainer is wandering about in the dark, what chance has the poor dog got? Dog training is like learning a language. It does not just happen. It requires the commitment to learn it backed up by solid hard work.

I must apologise to those of you who have read my book on training Hunter Pointer Retrievers, *The Versatile Gundog* (Sportsman's Press 1995) if you occasionally get a feeling of *déjà vue*. There are only so many ways to teach a dog to sit on its bum and the general principles of training a gundog remain pretty much the same from year to year. Indeed, a colleague pointed out that much of my 'original thinking' in *The Versatile Gundog* is also to be found in General Hutchinson's *Dog Breaking* published in 1848! However, *The Versatile Gundog* contains a lot more detail about the real 'nitty gritty' of the basic training and the three disciplines of hunting, pointing and retrieving than I have given space to here. In this book I have reiterated a number of points by way of emphasising their importance.

I have rather impersonally referred to the dog as 'it' to differentiate from 'he'/'she'/'they' the trainer except where a male dog or a bitch is specifically referred to. When referring to long distances I have assumed yards to equal the same length in metres.

Above all dog training should be FUN and if it is not fun for both trainer and pupil then something is very wrong somewhere. However, our dogs are usually very forgiving of our shortcomings. Indeed, they even sometimes appear to suffer fools gladly!

G.W.
The Warren, Llandefalle, Brecon

Introduction

If one turned the average six-month-old working-bred gundog loose in the wild – as, indeed, they still do with setters in some parts of Scandinavia and sled dogs in North America – there is no way that it would starve to death. It would hunt or point or retrieve *and eat* enough game to keep itself alive and well. It is only we humans who screw them up! A gundog has four legs whereas I only have two so it can run better than I can. It also has infinitely greater scenting powers than I shall ever have (notwithstanding a history of excessive nicotine intake!). Therefore, by and large, a gundog is far better equipped to find game than I am, which is basically why I use them. In many cases we use these qualities merely to increase our chances of putting game in the bag whereas in some cases, such as wildfowling or deerstalking, it is virtually criminal *not* to use a dog.

When acquiring a working dog for *any* job, be it hunting by scent, coursing, shepherding, police work or shooting, getting one of the right breed for the job in hand with the right breeding is more than half the battle. As ever, it is a question of 'Horses for Courses'. So once you have decided that you require the services of a trained dog (and, for better rather than worse, your sport will never be the same again) do not rush out and get hold of the first 'mutt' you come across but *stop and think*.

Do you go out sufficiently often to need a dog? Do you have the time to train or even look after a dog? Would you not be better off relying on the services of someone else's dog, e.g., the professional stalker, the goose guide, a hawking chum, the pointer handler or the pickers up? Might you not be better off buying a dog that is already trained? What is your main form of shooting? Do you also practise other forms of shooting or are you likely to do so in the future? Indeed, this book might almost be entitled *The Alternative Gundog* since many people require one dog to do more than one job. The person who shoots driven game on 50 days a year and stalks on 10 will obviously have a different requirement from the man stalking on 50 days and shooting driven game on only 10. However, in every case there are always several breeds of gundog capable of doing a combination of jobs although it should always be trained initially for its *primary* job and *kept solely for that particular activity for at least its FIRST season;* thereafter it can be introduced to other branches of your sport. (Unfortunately, the down side of this is that many dogs become wedded to their initial quarry and are less enthusiastic about some subsequent quarry species.) However, to try and teach it right from the start to do more than one job at once will only result in a thoroughly confused dog and, since you will have ten or twelve seasons work out of that dog, why ruin it for the sake of a few weeks sport?

The basic principles of teaching a pup to hunt or point or retrieve remain the same but the trainer will obviously slant the training towards the particular branch of sport for which that pup is destined. For example, teaching a dog to retrieve a wing-tipped duck from a fast flowing river necessarily requires a different technique to teaching it to retrieve the only pigeon in the decoy pattern that does *not* have a human hand scent on it. Both applications are, however, obviously still basically retrieving.

Apart from the working qualities that have been selectively bred into a particular breed of gundog for a particular job, the colour of a dog is frequently extremely important. (With regard to working ability there is absolutely *no* difference in colour although I still hear pundits proclaim such utter balderdash as 'No yellow Labrador can swim' or 'All black and white spaniels have a hard mouth' – usually based upon the first dog of that colour that they came across!) Stalking or wildfowling, for instance, require a neutral coloured dog to avoid detection by sharp eyed deer or wildfowl. There is no point in camouflaging yourself (these days almost literally) up to the eyeballs and having a dog next to you that stands out like the proverbial . . . The grouse hawker, however, requires a dog with a lot of white on it so that it *is* visible. As will be seen, there are ways round this like wearing a camouflage jacket but why make life difficult? On the other hand, with other forms of shooting the colour is immaterial and personal preference will often come into it (although it is a brave man who has the only yellow 'lab' out among a dozen anonymous black ones!) Incidentally, there is no such thing as a *golden* Labrador to a shooting man - they are always *yellow* whatever their actual colour; the term *golden* Labrador belongs purely to the showing and pet fraternity. (Golden retrievers are, of course, always golden retrievers.) As the horsemen say, though, 'No good horse is a bad colour.'

Size can also be important. When a dog is required to flounder through esturine mud for a goose and then swim back with it against an ebb tide or to work all day in tough, old knee-high heather or to pull down a wounded stag, then a good big'un will always beat a good littl'un. In other branches of one's sport, size may be immaterial and, again, a matter of personal choice but do not fall for the misconception that a smaller dog will be better in cover. It is the size of the dog's heart rather than its frame that will decide that one. Remember that male dogs are usually one third to a half larger than their sisters (working bred dogs are invariably much smaller and finer built than their heavier show bred counterparts).

I feel extremely strongly about the subject of breeding gundogs and I have included a chapter on the mechanics of breeding, but a few words on the subject here would not be out of place. Any professional gundog trainer will tell you that some dogs pretty well train themselves, are a delight to handle and make an excellent gundog at the end of it: with others, one puts in three times the work for only half the result. Those are the results of good and bad breeding respectively. Unfortunately there is more to breeding a good gundog than putting a good dog to a good bitch, neither of them necessarily a Field Trial Champion, and hey presto! That is only the start. Any racehorse breeder will tell you, several million pounds later, that putting the fastest stallion on the fastest mare will not guarantee producing the fastest foal. In each case that mating must 'nick' and it is difficult enough to produce the goods with two working bred gundogs of impeccable working ability and pedigrees without complicating the equation. With the exception of flatcoats and the minor spaniel breeds, all the *British* breeds of gundogs have two completely separate lines – showing and working – and never the twain should meet. Indeed, a working gundog and its show equivalent frequently appear to be almost two completely separate breeds. (In fact, these days one might be forgiven for thinking that we now almost have *three* types of gundog – showing, working and Field Trialling.) This situation has been accepted for over a century and each party is happy with the *status quo*. The Hunter Pointer Retrievers, on the other hand, are bred simultaneously for show and work but most attempts to breed a 'dual purpose' dog usually end up with an ugly looking dog that cannot work! I am frequently put in mind of a celebrated beauty of the day who wrote to Bernard Shaw proposing marriage saying, 'Imagine a child with my body and your brains.' Shaw responded with one of his famous postcard replies, 'Dear Madame, Imagine a child with my body and your brains. G.B.S.'! With HPRs the situation, brought about by an embarrassing lack of Field Trial awards in recent years, is starting to polarise and it may well be that the two parties will do the obvious thing and go their separate ways in the future.

However, having decided which breed will best suit your purpose(s) and having acquired your impeccably bred puppy (of which more later), it is up to you to bring out the best in that puppy for the job or jobs that it is required to do and that is what this book is all about. A gundog is like silage! The finished product can be no better than the original raw material but can be made worse in the process. Some years ago I was asked how many men I knew who shot superbly with an immaculately trained gundog. The list is still very short but I hope that this book will put one half right although I am unable to help you with the other - good luck!

'What happened next?' An apprehensive rabbit being pointed by a Hungarian wirehaired Vizsla.

PLATE 1

'The moment of truth': a GSP flushes a covey of grouse.

PLATE 2

Rabbit hawking with GSP and goshawk.

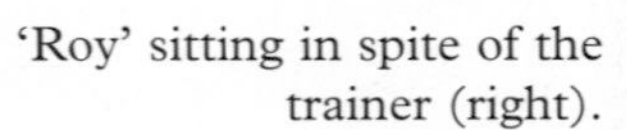

'Roy' sitting in spite of the trainer (right).

The author in 1989 on Thrumster, still one of the great dogging moors of Caithness.

1: 'Horses for Courses'

One man's meat is another man's poison Anon

For the tyro, there is a bewildering array of gundog breeds from which to choose. I am forever coming across people who have bought a completely unsuitable breed of dog for their purpose because they have not done their homework, have been badly advised by someone who either has pups to get rid of or is 'kennel blind' about his or her own particular breed, or they have had preconceived ideas based on nothing from which they will not shift. In every case the poor dog comes off second best and the owner is disillusioned. In this chapter I have set out my *personal* opinions of each breed insofar as one can generalise about any breed of gundog (which is akin to saying that *all* British people are reserved and *all* Italians are volatile!) I have omitted a detailed history of each breed which is already well documented in many other gundog books. I have also included a table giving *my* marks from 0-5 for each breed's suitability for a particular job. I must stress that these are *personal* opinions based on training well over a thousand gundogs of just about every conceivable breed for every conceivable job and then putting it into practice over more than twenty years. Whenever one sticks one's head over the parapet someone is always going to shoot at you and everyone is going to jump up and down with 'one of such-and-such a breed that did such-and-such a job far better than one of a so-&-so breed'. I would not argue but 'one swallow . . ' And I can only generalise.

The bottom line is that a gundog is a dog bred to have game killed over it with a gun. This is why they look like they do, why they behave like they do and what, for more than two centuries, they have been selectively bred to do. (At the risk of stating the obvious, this is why cairn terriers, whippets or bulldogs for example do not look like or make very good gundogs!) All gundogs fall into one of four categories: Spaniels; Retrievers; Pointers and Setters (or 'Bird Dogs' to use the American term) and the continental Hunter Pointer Retrievers (HPRs for short). Spaniels are bred to hunt and to retrieve, retrievers are bred to retrieve, pointers and setters are bred to hunt and to point while HPRs are bred to hunt, to point and to retrieve. Granted, they can all frequently be trained to do other jobs as well but these are their *raison d'être* which should help one to make ones initial choice.

All breeds of working bred gundogs (and these are the only sort with which we shall concern ourselves from now on) should have certain characteristics in common irrespective of their role. They should have excellent 'noses' or scenting powers for air and/or ground scent, they should have soft mouths when retrieving from land or water, they should be (vocally) quiet while working, they should have the desire to find live, dead or wounded game as the case may be, they should have 'trainability' or the will to obey the wishes of their trainer, they should be physically sound and capable of doing a day's work and, possibly above all, they should be a pleasure to own, to work and generally to have around the place with adults, children and other dogs. All of which sounds pretty obvious until one looks at what passes for a gundog among one's friends and shooting colleagues! (Fortunately, virtually every working bred gundog of any breed or age that I have ever come across has been 100% good with children and has let 'ankle biters' do things that no adult would ever get away with.)

Whereas we all hope for the best in a dog and try to train it to the best of our abilities I would go so far as to say that *the absolutely perfect gundog has yet to be produced* although, for a multitude of reasons, some naturally come closer to the ideal than others.

SPANIELS

The bustling, energetic and (hopefully) close hunting workers of the gundog world that also retrieve. They can also be persuaded to perform more sedentary tasks (much against their will!). One of the great post-war gundog trainers said that 50% of spaniels need pep pills and the other 50% need hearing aids – and not a lot has changed since! Their undoubted popularity stems from being relatively easy to train (although after some of the sights seen out shooting one might query this) and extremely effective hunters as well as being efficient retrievers.

English Springer Spaniel (ESS) Too well-known to require description they come in liver and white (L/W) and black and white (B/W). Their size varies from almost Jack Russell size up to a small Labrador but the larger ones are less common these days. Their coats are also a lot finer than they used to be. They are one of the two most popular gundog breeds in Britain today (the other, of course, being the Labrador) and probably best described by Peter Moxon's words, 'The Maid of All Work'. Hunting is their forte and the thicker the cover, the more they like it (or ought to!). The spaniel and the rabbit seem to be made for one another although most other varieties of game do not come amiss either. They should hunt well within gunshot range of their handler, flush quarry and retrieve it from land or water when shot. They are excellent retrievers over relatively short distances i.e. up to 100 yards. I frequently find that the more a springer enjoys hunting, the less keen it is on retrieving and *vice versa* but one is obviously hoping for one that does both with equal enthusiasm as many do. They may be trained purely as retrievers but essentially they are *busy* dogs and at their best when ferreting about in the undergrowth and on the move.

Cocker These 'wee doggies' have made a great comeback over the last two decades from being almost a minor breed. Over a century ago when specific breeds were being evolved, any small spaniels in a litter became cockers and their larger siblings were designated springers. However, nowadays you are most definitely not getting a diminutive springer! Their colours include black, liver, chocolate, roan, golden, orange and white (O/W), L/W and B/W. A litter of springers generally has some puppies of *average* working ability; there is no such thing an *average* cocker pup. A springer in training has a gradual learning curve whereas that of a cocker is akin to a game of Snakes and Ladders! A friend describes training a cocker like bringing up a bright but naughty child but they do have an undeniable charm all of their own. Having said all that, they are little hunting machines with great game sense although they would sooner hunt from one likely patch of cover to the next rather than quarter in the 'windscreen wiper' mode, are excellent in cover and I have frequently seen them retrieve quarry almost as big as themselves. One theory is that their name derives from dogs for woodcock work.

RETRIEVERS

The dependable stalwarts that primarily stay beside their handler until required to retrieve but can also be taught to do a number of other jobs as well.

Labrador Retriever (lab) The other favourite British shooting dog. A client once told me that if one could not train a Labrador, one should not own a dog! My senior Labrador (lying by my feet as I type) will sit beside me on any 200 bird day to which I am lucky enough to be invited, hunt like a spaniel in the brambles on a Stand-'n'-Drive day, stalk deer with me and point woodcock – and I cannot ever recall actually training her! She is also terribly boring, bless her, compared with some of my hooligans! Labradors come in black, yellow – varying from almost white to a deep russet – and chocolate (a genetic mix of black and yellow) although working bred chocolate labs are about as common as the proverbial rocking horse droppings. Labradors are extremely easy to train - indeed, it has been said that a Labrador is born half-trained and a spaniel dies half-trained! They *ought* to have an almost phlegmatic temperament, will sit beside one or walk to heel indefinitely and are excellent retrievers. For these reasons they are the premier choice for the covert shooter and one day I shall make my fortune by inventing an inflatable rubber black 'lavatory door' that guns can blow up and sit beside their pegs during the drive! Labs also adore water, can be taught to hunt (although a lab will only go into cover if it *knows* that there is something there, whereas a spaniel will go in on the off chance that there *might* be something there) and a lot of grouse men use them on 'the hill' for hunting because of their size, constitution and length of leg. Many labs take easily to deerstalking but since no-one has ever specifically bred a line of stalking Labradors, one is always taking pot luck in that department however good their ancestors may be on game, and it is extremely difficult to get them to give tongue on a dead or wounded deer. Labradors bred in Scotland seem more deer-orientated than their southern cousins. At the risk of upsetting 'The First Lady of Falconry' they are useless for falconry! A few Labradors will point (in the United States they have developed lines of pointing Labradors) although, like most breeds, one can tell the presence of game by the dog's individual body language. (Body language, incidentally, is a much underestimated characteristic in any gundog and will tell the handler a lot in many instances if he has the wit to look for it. Other trainers absorb it unconsciously and only notice it when it is absent.) My wife maintains that Labradors are a lot easier to have in the house than any other gundog breed, although as guard dogs they are pretty pathetic!

Golden Retriever The working bred goldens tend to be a pleasing deep foxy red (as opposed to the custard cream colour of the more heavily built show dogs). My parents always had goldens and, as a boy, I got up to a lot of mischief with 'Bruce' and a folding, single barrel .410! Although relatively uncommon compared with labs, they have their devotees who have frequently demonstrated that they can hold their own with any black job in the field. I have seen some excellent goldens in action and in every respect they are capable of performing the same tasks as any Labrador.

Flatcoated Retriever I always think of a flatcoat as 'an Edwardian Gentleman' and I have owned some extremely good ones. They are either black or occasionally liver and were almost certainly evolved from the old North American 'retriever', setter and collie. A century ago there was a hotch potch of black retrievers developed from the 'Newfoundland retrievers' and various outcrosses. Eventually these were designated separate breeds purely from their coat texture within the same litter and became flatcoats, curly coats, Labradors etc and many labs still have an almost curly coat today. Flatcoats are the only *serious* British gundog breed to be simultaneously worked and shown and they are definitely the Peter Pans of the gundog world. They are extremely slow to mature and some just never quite seem to ever grow up! The setter in them makes many of them natural pointers and they are great hunters in cover. In Edwardian times they were far more popular than the Labradors but their popularity started to wane after the First World War. The people who kept them going were the professional gamekeepers who used them both to hunt and to pick up. My own personal theory is that their decline in popularity coincided with the new fashion for keeping working gundogs in the home as a pet. When a flatcoat moults, by gosh it moults and whoever was responsible for cleaning soon put their foot down. The gamekeepers, meanwhile, continued to keep them in kennels so moulting was never a problem. If you have a good flatcoat you would never need another dog!

Chesapeake Bay Retriever (Chessie, pronounced chezzie) These are, above all, the ultimate wildfowling dog. With their dun colour they are ideally camouflaged for the saltings, their thick two-layered oily coat makes them impervious to the iciest water, their large robust frames and almost webbed feet enable them to be tireless swimmers. They have a natural affinity with waterfowl and their ability to account for a wounded, diving duck is almost inherent. They are the 'lager louts' of the retriever world but the best will hold their own with a Labrador at the covertside and, judging by some of the horror stories that have come my way, I can think of no better beast for tackling a wounded sika stag! They appear to be less easy to train than other retrievers, many require firm handling and they have a reputation for being one-man dogs.

Nova Scotia Duck Tolling Retriever *(to give it its full name and title – otherwise known as 'Duck Tollers!)* These are spaniel-sized, thick russet-coated, bushy-tailed, pointed-muzzled, prick-eared foxy-looking varmints – which is exactly what they are supposed to look like. They are bred to resemble a fox and their antics on the shore line were used to draw inquisitive wildfowl within range of the mammoth fowling pieces – almost shoulder-mounted punt guns – of the 'market gunners' a century and more ago. The duck tollers would then retrieve the slain waterfowl for sale in the meat hungry cities of the north-eastern American seaboard the following morning. (Similar looking dogs, known as 'pipers', were also bred over here to entice wildfowl into the 'pipes', or netted tunnels, of decoy ponds by dodging in and out of reed screens or 'yacoups'.) I, personally, have not had much success with the few that I have had in to train.

The difference between working a spaniel or a retriever on the one hand and a pointing dog on the other is that the former two are master/servant relationships with the dog always under direct control of its handler; with a pointing dog, the relationship eventually becomes a partnership with the dog frequently working out of sight of the handler and the handler trusting the dog to do its job unaided. For this reason I tell anyone new to pointing dogs to forget anything that they ever knew about spaniels or retrievers!

POINTERS and SETTERS

'Bird dogs' are the thoroughbreds of the gundog world as they flow effortlessly over the heather, roots or stubble in a single-minded quest to detect the merest whiff of game scent with those exquisite air-scenting noses. They can be taught to hunt in cover and throughout the rest of the world they are also expected to retrieve any game shot over them. They are completely feather orientated and should ignore fur. Although in theory their season in Britain should last from the Glorious Twelfth until the end of January, in practice most of them have a relatively short working season every year.

Pointer Nowadays often incorrectly called 'English' Pointers to distinguish them from the German Pointers. B/W, L/W or O/W, they are numerically the most popular of the Bird Dogs and they are extremely easy to train. Indeed, if bred right, one only has to teach them to turn and to drop as the ruthless selective breeding carried out by our forefathers has seen to the rest of it! The large amount of white on them enables them to be easily seen against the heather when on point and, if allowed to drink regularly, they will hunt in the hottest of weather due to their fine coats. 'Their sensitivity,' to quote the late John Nash from County Limerick who made up 47 Field Trial Champion Pointers, Irish Setters and English Springers, 'is the braking system on the 100 horse power machine.' With finely-tuned noses for air scent they are bred to range widely at the gallop over vast areas of sparsely stocked moorland in search of grouse, snipe and woodcock or to quarter the lowland stubbles and root fields for partridges and, nowadays, often pheasant. Grouse, however, is their real speciality and the sight of any pointing dog suddenly slamming on point on a covey ought to send shivers up the spine of any true dog man. Apart from shooting dogs, when they should be accompanied by a retriever walking at heel to collect the shot game, they are the ideal dog for game hawking under longwings, either for grouse hawking with a peregrine falcon or for partridge hawking with a tiercel. (I cannot comment on the current fashion for merlin/gyr etc. hybrids.) Although in Great Britain they are not expected to collect shot game, I allow my own pointers to retrieve after their second shooting season. Over here, though, their job technically finishes with the drop to flush, which is a bit like *coitus interruptus* for the poor dog!

English Setter Long haired with a lot of 'feather', they are essentially white with lemon, brown or black markings and many are ticked or flecked. The red or blue and sometimes yellow 'belton' (similar to 'roan' in a horse) is also common. They are less forgiving than pointers of training errors by their handler and they operate far better in cold, wet climates. They seem to need game experience much earlier on in training than a pointer. Most of the flat dogging estates of Caithness and Sutherland prefer setters which, in addition to grouse, have a natural affinity for the snipe and woodcock which come in in large falls on the September, October and November moons respectively from more northern climes. Many of the eminent pre-war falconers preferred English setters to pointers but we have since exported most of our best ones all over the world. Many setters still lie down when 'setting' which dates from their original (pre-firearms) use which entailed nets being drawn over them to put coveys of partridges in the pot.

One cannot mention English setters without mentioning the Llewellin setters which are virtually a separate breed - almost a sub-species of English setter. Llewellin setters were originally bred by one Edward Laverack from a brother/sister mating of two near-perfect siblings in the early nineteenth century and then line bred for the next fifty years without an outcross. On his death in 1877, the Laverack setters were taken over by his friend Purcel Llewellin who, by judicious setter outcrossing, produced setters with all the 'go' of the Laveracks but a lot easier to handle. These dogs then became the Llewellin setters that are still famous the world over.

Irish Setter (Red Setter) As the name suggests, a deep mahogany colour or red and white. Although all Irish setters were originally red and white, a fashion for solid red setters developed and recently the show fraternity have both revived and equally quickly ruined the modern red and white Irish setter. Today's working Irish setters have been bred to run for several hours for a single point on a snipe in a land where game is very scarce. Whether it is because of, or in spite of this, that the Irish invaders continue to come over year after year and sweep the board at our Field Trials I know not! No wonder that their dogs have a great hunger for finding game and they seem to conjure up game where none apparently exists. Most Irish setters appear to be far more forgiving of 'pilot error' or clumsy treatment than their English counterparts. As the rabbit is to the spaniel and the grouse is to the pointer, so is the snipe to the 'red dogs'. Although their colour makes it more difficult for a falconer to see the dog on point when he is concentrating on his falcon, it is an oft proven fact that, when birds are jumpy, a dark coloured dog can approach a lot closer to game than a white one (as long as the party is sombrely dressed, does not 'crowd' the game and *keeps quiet*!).

Gordon Setter As a former Gordon Highlander I have a soft spot for the Gordons. The 'Black and Tan' setters (occasionally tri-colours crop up) attributed to the Fourth Duke of Gordon are slow to mature but of the small percentage running in present day Field Trials, a large percentage of the prizes are scooped by them. They have their devotees but are numerically the least of the three setter breeds. Apart from their traditional role of grouse finders in the Grampians they are splendid rough shooting dogs and the majority are natural retrievers.

HUNTER POINTER RETRIEVER (HPR)

These are the newly imported (since the 1950s) exotics that are expected to hunt, point, retrieve, drive the car, carry the gun etc., etc., and generally do it all. Because more is expected of them than the British breeds, they often fall down on one of these disciplines and have long been called Jack of all trades. They are definitely not all things to all men but are excellent rough shooting dogs on either low or high ground and at their best over large areas containing little game, splendid assistants to an austringer (as the man who flies short-winged hawks is known) and will also do the true falconer's job; most of the

German dogs are extremely deer orientated. They should work on both fur and feather. Their decriers have long labelled them as 'hard-mouthed, whingeing brutes' and sometimes with due cause. Considering that the German breeds have been bred for generations to pull down wounded boar, foxes and even wolves I am forever surprised that so many have such soft mouths, particularly when one bears in mind that hard mouth is not considered a major fault in Germany. They have also been bred to bay dead or wounded boar and deer and if one breeds for 'voice', one often gets more 'voice' than one wants. Hardmouthed or 'vocal' dogs of *any* breed should *never* be bred from and these faults are often unknowingly induced by bad training or even bad upbringing. HPRs are very slow to mature and most do not come into their own much before their second or even third working season. Indeed, if I had an English springer and, say, a GSP born on the same day I would be shooting over that springer before I had even started to train the GSP. Their full working potential will only really be completely realised when those who work them *only* work them and those who show them stick to showing them, with both parties thereafter go their separate ways like every other gundog breed in Britain. Apart from the breeds that I have mentioned below, there are numerous 'sports', variations etc. of these breeds: Longhaired Weimaraners, wirehaired vizslas, German longhaired pointers etc. etc. Take them as you will . . .

German Shorthaired Pointer (GSP) Solid liver, solid black, L/W ticked, B/W ticked. Most are well camouflaged (although those without the ticking are the colour of a springer!) Numerically the strongest, they are among the easiest of the HPRs to train and are extremely versatile. Yesterday I took a 5-year-old GSP bitch deerstalking before taking her beating on a pheasant shoot. I was asked to pick up on the first drive out of root crops and for the rest of the morning she went beating with gusto in particularly thick brambles (but I did not teach her all these trades at once.) They are excellent dogs on 'the hill' and, with experience, will also work downwind like a long range spaniel when grouse are driven. As with most HPRs they are effective snipe and woodcock dogs. Like all the German HPRs they are very good at woodland deerstalking although, like Weimaraners, their thin, fine coats make them more suitable for stalking in the kinder climate of southern Britain. GSPs tend to be either wimps or hooligans with little in between. They are extremely athletic and energetic which can sometimes be a mixed blessing! They adore their owners and, in common with other HPRs, dislike being separated from them which is the 'down' side of the partnership. However, if correctly handled from puppyhood, this can easily be overcome. They are at their best when on the move rather than sitting by pegs or in pigeon hides.

German Wirehaired Pointer (GWP, 'Wirehair') If GSPs can be hooligans, wirehairs can be delinquents if not downright thugs! The same colours as

GSPs, they are one of the pointing griffon breeds bred for performance, stamina and coat texture, although the last varies considerably. The modern GWPs in Britain are not quite as 'hard' in their character as twenty years ago but many are not quite as 'hard' in their work either. They are both mentally and physically extremely tough and quick to take advantage of any weakness in their handler. In equestrian terms, 'Not a novice ride!' Both sexes can be noisy and be stroppy with other dogs of the same sex. However, they will form a great rapport with any trainer who can command their respect and are extremely capable performers with a great hunger for finding game. When I first coined the phrase 'Life to a dog is either black or white' I was applying it to GWPs! If it appears that I am damning them out of hand, when asked what dog I would have if restricted to only one dog, I always say it would have to be a male 'wirehair' dog. Not that they are any better than, or that I prefer them to, any others but simply because they would be the most capable of doing the large amount of stalking, falconry, driven and walked up game shooting that I am fortunate enough to practise.

Weimaraner (Weimar, 'Grey Ghost') Originally bred from the hounds of the Saint Hubert monastery in the Ardennes, the Weimar is essentially still a hound that has been evolved into a combination of gundog and guard dog. They are low scenting dogs, hunting at a slower pace and with a lower head carriage than most pointing dogs. They are excellent deer dogs and although only a small proportion of the many Weimaraners in the UK are actually worked in the shooting field, I have come across very few bad ones. They are less stylish than most other HPR breeds but are very thorough. They tend to be one man dogs, difficult feeders, are usually antisocial with other breeds, do not like being in strange kennels and they feel the cold. However they are excellent guard dogs and very capable performers in the field. It is as well to remember that they get easily bored during early training.

Large Munsterlander ('Munster') Best described as a 'collie coloured setter' to look at, the Munster is a much underestimated gundog having a lot of natural ability and great game sense. They hunt with great style and their penchant for trying to take in too much ground makes them naturals for the hill. They will hunt, point and retrieve naturally, are good stalking dogs and can be worked under longwings or shortwings. Like Weimars, they can be difficult feeders and do not always do well in strange kennels. Many of them unfortunately 'witter' – again, a breeding fault.

Hungarian Vizsla (Golden Pointer, 'Whizzle') The colour of dead bracken, these russet-coloured descendants of the yellow hunting dogs from Turkey that swept into central Europe with the Magyar hordes are the true allrounders. They easily adapt to any job that requires all three HPR disciplines. Shooting, deer work and falconry all come alike to them. They suit sensitive trainers but do not be fooled by the grovelling when ticked off! Many actually have a very stubborn streak through them but, like many sensitive dogs, can be kidded into doing what is required by a roundabout training route rather than by a direct confrontation. (This does not mean that they should be allowed to get away with it)

Brittany ('Brit') These cobby, little short-tailed (or tail-less) pointing spaniels from north west France are 'huntaholics'. Originally called Brittany Spaniels the latter word has now been officially dropped in the UK. They come in a variety of colours with B/W, O/W & tricolour being the most common. They hunt a lot wider than our native spaniels and many are not natural retrievers. I have long suspected that in France and in America (whence many were taken by returning GIs and where they are now extremely popular) they are automatically taught to 'force retrieve' – a method that involves a certain amount of pain but produces compulsory retrievers. They are not naturals in thick cover but, like all gundogs, can be effectively taught to enter cover from an early age. If required for shooting – and woodcock is their forte – the trainer would be advised to teach them to retrieve *interesting* objects before introducing them to the joys of hunting. Brits will take as much hunting as you can throw at them – and then a bit more! They are excellent dogs for shortwinged, broadwinged and Harris hawks, being natural pointers, but their relatively short legs preclude them from serious grouse work. I, personally, have yet to come across one that was any good for deerstalking.

Italian Spinone Most of the originally imported spinoni (plural!) came from predominantly show kennels in Italy so they have been slow to catch on here with sportsmen and women. They have been described as a 'Hoover on four legs' and, covering the ground with their unique trotting gait, are reputed to miss nothing in the way of game and they have a very weatherproof coat. A number of falconers swear by them and I know of some excellent rough shooting spinoni but I, personally, have not had a lot to do with them.

Bracco Italiano Another Italian HPR , this time with a smooth coat. A popular all-rounder in Italy but there are relatively few in Britain.
It seems almost certain that now the quarantine laws have been relaxed we can expect to see further new breeds of continental gundogs such as the Kooikerhondje coming over as well as different bloodlines being imported to improve the existing breeds. (A few years ago less than 200 working English setters were registered in UK while several thousand of them were registered in Italy!)

Minor Breeds

I am a great supporter of anyone who attempts to revive the working ability of the minor breeds which has been bred out of them by exhibiting them at dog shows. However, I have excluded them from my comments because their lack of working ability is the reason why they *are* now minor breeds in the shooting world. It is difficult enough to get a decent working gundog of good working parentage and I feel that it would be misleading to novice trainers to give the impression that they would have an equal chance of success with one of the minor breeds. I still maintain, though, that someone will always get on better with a breed that he or she likes and wants.

These include - Spaniels: Welsh Springer, Clumber, Sussex and Field. Retrievers: Curly coated and the Irish Water Spaniel (now classified as retrievers). They all have their devotees and jolly good luck to them.

Nor should one ever turn up ones nose at the chance of a crossbred gundog if *both* parents are of working stock (for that is how all our recognised gundog breeds were evolved 100 years ago.) If they cross breed themselves you often get the best of both worlds, but if you cross breed them intentionally ... 'Sprockers', 'Spandors', 'Retrieverdors', 'Labollies' and 'Pointerdors' (to name but a few) have frequently outperformed their bluer-blooded cousins and they have the advantage of being considerably cheaper as puppies to boot. (I have a theory that 75% of the mongrels in Britain are sired by Labradors, Border collies or Jack Russells!)

Below is my own *personal* chart of the aforementioned breeds' suitability for each job. 'Yer pays yer money and yer takes yer choice...'

	Walked up Grouse	Driven Grouse Picking-Up	Driven Grouse Beating	Snipe	Wildfowling	Woodcock	Pigeon Shooting	Deerstalking	Falconry, Longwings	Falconry, Shortwings	Roughshooting	Covershooting	Picking-Up	Beating
English Springer Spaniel	3	4	3	5	3	5	5	2	0	3	5	3	5	5
Cocker Spaniel	2	3	2	4	2	5	4	3	0	3	5	3	5	5
Labrador	4	5	5	5	5	3	5	4	0	1	3	5	5	4
Golden Retriever	3	5	4	5	5	3	5	4	0	1	3	5	5	4
Flatcoat	3	5	4	5	5	3	5	4	0	1	3	5	5	4
Chesapeake Bay Retriever	2	5	3	4	5	2	5	5	0	0	3	4	4	3
Pointer	5	0	1	5	0	5	0	0	5	2	1	0	0	0
English Setter	5	0	1	5	0	5	0	0	5	2	3	0	0	0
Irish Setter	5	0	1	5	0	5	0	0	5	2	3	0	0	0
Gordon Setter	5	0	1	5	0	5	0	0	5	2	3	0	0	0
German Shorthaired Pointer	4	3	5	3	3	4	3	5	3	5	5	1	3	3
German Wirehaired Pointer	4	3	4	5	3	4	3	5	3	5	5	1	3	3
Weimaraner	4	3	5	5	3	4	3	5	3	5	5	1	3	3
Large Munsterlander	4	3	4	5	3	4	3	5	3	5	5	1	3	3
Vizsla	4	3	5	5	3	4	3	5	3	5	5	1	3	3
Brittany	3	1	3	5	1	5	1	1	2	5	3	0	1	3

2: First Things First

Where there's a will, there's a way. Anon.

Having decided that you both want and need a working gundog it should fulfil several requirements. It should be capable of doing the job or jobs required of it on the terrain where you operate. It should fit into your own lifestyle and situation 365 days a year and it should be from a breed that you like and want. That established, there are still a number of factors to consider in some depth before taking the plunge. They are all in the form of simple questions and generally they all have simple answers but they must be asked all the same. Do you have the necessary time to look after, let alone train and work, a dog? Will you be capable of training and handling a dog? How many dogs should you have? A male dog or a bitch? Have you discussed it with the other members of the household? Are any of them allergic to or frightened of dogs? Are they to be involved with it as a family pet cum gundog or will it be entirely 'your pigeon' as a working dog. If you go away on a regular basis who will look after it in your absence? Do you live in a suitable place for owning a working dog both as an individual property and as a general area? Will it live indoors or in a kennel? How much exercise does it need? What will it be fed on? What is the best time of year in which to get the dog? All these questions have to be addressed in detail and answered thoroughly before you go any further. One is reminded of the man who asked 'How much does it cost to feed a dog?' to which the breeder replied 'Then you obviously cannot afford one'! The canine version of the car sticker saying 'A Turkey is for Christmas, not for life' also applies to gundogs.

Answering the foregoing questions in order, the average adult gundog requires a minimum of twenty minutes in the morning and half an hour at night. Only time will tell whether you can handle a dog and some dogs are much easier to handle than others. You will know, but your friends will not tell you. (If you tell any man he cannot drive a car, train a dog or make love you have a serious problem on your hands!). Any novice trainer should only ever have one pupil or he will end up with two half-trained dogs. However, if kennelled for long periods, some dogs benefit from having a non-working 'mutt' as a companion and it keeps the rest of the family from meddling with your gundog! They may both be exercised together but never forget that more than one dog is a pack and they will look to one another rather than to you. Dog or bitch? There is an old saying that 'a bitch is a nuisance for six weeks of the year but a dog is a nuisance every damned day' and *most* bitches work to please their owner whereas *most* dogs work to please their blasted selves. The other side of the coin is that I took a pointer bitch and her two daughters up to Scotland for the grouse and all three came in season for three weeks on the 11th, the Glorious Twelfth and the 13th of August! A male dog has a lot more work in him than a bitch and for deerstalking is bigger, more persevering on a difficult blood trail and more likely to 'mix it' with a wounded deer. Strong characters generally get on better with male dogs while others get on better with bitches.

One should discuss it thoroughly with one's other half: dumping a surprise bundle of fluff into his or her lap sometimes backfires! As life gets further and further away from nature I, personally, feel that young children should have some contact with animals When our daughter was four months old my wife and I moved into a caravan alongside a derelict farmhouse with no water, electricity or telephone and brought with us three litters of puppies which were installed in makeshift runs outside – but I cannot honestly recommend it! However, I have never for the life of me been able to understand the connection between having a baby and not keeping a dog. People are sometimes allergic to dogs (and doesn't the diagnosis take forever?) which precludes having a dog *inside* the house but a dog kennelled outside does not usually pose a problem and a young puppy is an excellent way of getting someone over a phobia about dogs. To what extent the rest of one's family should be involved is always a difficult one. It is no coincidence that most indifferent retrievers from recognised retrieving breeds invariably come from families with small children. It is certainly essential that the whole family use the same words of command. If *he* uses 'HUP' and *she* uses 'SIT' but she uses 'HUP' to get Fido into the car . . . the best compromise is that the family's involvement is limited to within the house and garden and if the dog is taken for a walk it is *always* on a lead. This is where the 'mutt' comes in. Any dog's allegiance is to whoever gives it its free-running exercise/work irrespective of who feeds it. Any household pet be it dog, cat or goldfish requires a certain amount of regular daily attention. If one is single, making a car cage in ones car as its second home has a lot of advantages. If one has a co-operative 'significant other' (or even a wife or husband!) the problem is more easily solved.

Any gundog trainer needs an area of grass as the bare minimum on which to train their dog and the trainer with a house and garden and 'a field out at the back' obviously has great advantages over the man in a high-rise tower block. Some Local Authorities are also becoming more and more pernickety over perceived dog-related Public Health problems. (I have just read that the 'Beautification Office' in Fuzhou, a coastal city in Southern China, has ordered every inhabitant to destroy their pet dogs within 14 days.) However, a pointer Field Trialler in New York keeps his dogs on his twentieth-storey balcony, his training pigeons in a box on the skyscraper wall and his Bob White quail above the kennel. He trains in Central Park at 5 am every morning and wins a lot of trials. A gamekeeper friend in North Wales used to drive a 36 mile round trip every evening to train his spaniel when he was a carworker at Longbridge.

As soon as a gundog starts living in the house as a family pet, its training is straightaway compromised. There are too many distractions. I firmly believe that the best, nay the only, way to keep a working gundog is to have an outside kennel and run as its *primary* home and to have it with you when it suits *you.* That does not mean leaving a young pup to stagnate in its kennel and to grow up 'kennel shy' (of which more later) but when a young dog starts its 4-6 month training period it should be confined to kennels 24 hours a day, except for a 10 minute scamper in the morning and a 10 minute scamper in the evening before training. If that pup is playing with the children and chasing rabbits down the hedge all day and you haul it onto the lawn in the evening and tell it to 'Sit on its bum', that pup will think that life is far more fun when playing with the kids and chasing rabbits and will be mentally exhausted by the evening anyway. (Try giving your primary school child an unpopular order when just off the school bus after a long day!) If, however, that pup is looking at four bare walls all day and you haul it onto the lawn in the evening and tell it to 'Sit on its bum', the pup will much prefer being trained to looking at those four walls. In addition, that little brain will be completely uncluttered and will act as a little sponge to absorb everything that you tell it. Unfortunately it is *people* and their egos who firmly believe that a dog should have human company 24 hours a day. They have never asked the dog! If, for whatever reason, you *must* have the dog in the house, then make or buy a (preferably) solid-sided car cage such as the Lintran that is large enough to eventually hold the pup when an adult, put it where it is least in the way and make that its kennel. It gives the dog the all-important territorial security, keeps it from under everyone's feet and prevents it from chewing up the happy home when you are not there. Confining the dog to the porch or utility room in lieu of a kennel is just about an acceptable compromise.

Beware the Great British Myth that every dog needs 'a good long walk' every day. *It does not.* I have never taken a dog for a walk in my life If you wish to go for a walk then do so by all means – *but leave the dog at home.* Young pups need a number of ten minute scampers at regular intervals followed by crashing out, increasing to a twenty minute scamper *under close supervision* morning and evening as they get older – and that is all a working gundog will ever need for the rest of its life! There is a very definite difference between 'controlled exercise' when ones total concentration is on that dog and a 'walk' which usually involves a pram, two other kids, the family Jack Russell and a lot of gossiping while ones pupil is creating mayhem unseen out of range and out of control!

Although I am a great fan of raw tripe and raw flesh for dogs, this method of feeding is beset by problems. A 20 kg bag of 'complete' or 'all-in' dog food will last the average adult gundog 4-8 weeks, is excellent value for money, convenient to use and will keep the dog in excellent health. Forget tinned 'meat' (nearly all water) and biscuits which, in my opinion, are a complete waste of money even though most dogs get by on most dog foods. I often think of the rubbish that was fed to foxhounds during the War when nothing else was available and they were still hunting three days a week and galloping 60 miles a day!

Since *as a generalisation* one starts seriously training a spaniel at 6-8 months old, a retriever at 8-10 months old and a pointing dog at 10-12 months old, the pup wants to be that age in March-May so that you have the long summer evenings in which to train it. So get out your calculator and work backwards from there as to when you buy your 7 week-old-pup according to the breed.

So, in an ideal world (which seldom seems to exist!) your pup is kennelled in án outside kennel and run, fed on a 'complete' dog food, takes up 20 minutes morning and 30 minutes evening, is exercised in the field behind the house, the children leave it alone and your other half looks after it when you are away. In return you have a lot of fun and end up with a steady, biddable shooting companion who is also a great friend (note the word 'who'!) Not a bad deal!

3: Confined to Quarters

A kennel is the greatest training aid of them all. Bryan Gough.

Anyone training a gundog seriously must accept that once the pupil is beyond a certain age it is *never* left to its own devices but is either confined or being trained. Any deviation from this principle will assuredly result in a Mickey Mouse gundog. Therefore one must work out from the outset whether one wants a 'trained gundog' or a family pet that is a 'kind of a sort of a gundog.' Confining the dog ensures that one's pupil is physically prevented from doing its own thing and so getting up to any mischief that would be counter-productive to its training. It may be chained to a 'Fido' kennel, kept in a traditional kennel and run, kept in the utility room or even shut in the car at times. No kennel is expected to be large enough to actually exercise a dog but is used in conjunction with regular free running but closely supervised exercise outside.

KENNELS

Having decided to kennel your dog, it makes sense to give it the best you can manage because the dog (and its eventual successors) will spend a lot of time in that kennel. In America many working gundogs are kept on a chain with access to a suitable kennel whereas in Britain it is mainly working sheepdogs (Border collies), lurchers and bulldogs in *Tom and Jerry* cartoons that are kept thus. Many firms manufacturing wooden, galvanised metal and 'composite' kennels suitable for gundogs advertise in the Sporting and Canine press and by and large you get what you pay for. Many other owners make their own or adapt existing buildings but any kennel should meet several criteria It should be large enough for the dog(s) to move around in comfortably; strong enough to be both escape *and* entry proof, i.e. chew proof and capable of being thoroughly cleaned. It should ideally be sectional and consequently movable, it should admit plenty of light and air and the sleeping compartment should be damp free and draught free and therefore comfortable. In the northern half of Britain colder, wetter weather and heavy snowfalls should also be considered. Where bad weather, noise or nearby distractions is a factor, a run covered on three sides and roofed over with just the front open may be better than a conventional run. In a small garden an L-shaped kennel and run may fit better and falconers should consider siting the kennel adjacent to the mews to give the added security of a guard dog. 'Out of sight is out of mind' and with some kennels tucked away down the garden one must be careful not to virtually ignore the dogs existence and let it stagnate. I do not allow kennelled dogs to wear collars. I have seen too many accidents happen as a result (some of them fatal)

Not a classical stance, but this dog of the author's never told a lie.

PLATE 3

Young pointer in the training pen. Having live game to hand certainly helps.

The irresistible force meets the immovable object.

PLATE 4

Voilà! The point (GSP on a wingclipped hen pheasant).

especially when more than one dog is kennelled.

The kennel should preferably face south or south east. A 4 x 4 ft (1.25 m x 1.25 m) kennel and 8 x 4 ft (2.5 m x 1.25 m) run is large enough for one or two large gundogs or three spaniel-sized dogs (two dogs do not need twice the room of one dog and you can always put one or more small dogs in a large kennel but not one or more large dogs in a small kennel). If the frame of the run is made of wood, the weldmesh should be stapled to the *inside* of the frame which inhibits chewing. If you have a 'carpenter' paint the chewed parts with a mixture of diesel and creosote/Jeyes Fluid and then tack on offcuts of *untreated* white deal which can be replaced as necessary. The run needs to be high enough to avoid stooping when it is roofed over. The sleeping kennel itself is warmer if it has a wooden floor and the walls are lined with plywood or sterling board so there are no edges for a bored dog to chew. A hinged false roof about 3 ft (1 m) high in a 6 ft (2 m) high kennel makes it warmer in winter. The bench area size is dictated by the size of the dog(s) curled up rather than standing up or stretched out. A wooden beer barrel or plastic carboy with a few small holes drilled in the bottom for drainage, lying on its side on a wooden cradle with the open end at right angles to the entrance hole makes a very snug bed. The whole kennel and run should be on a 3 in. (75 cm) concrete pad or 2 ft (600 cm) square concrete slabs laid with 2 in. (50 cm) gaps filled with a sand/cement (5:1) mix and sprinkled with water to form an impervious base under which urine cannot seep. A slight fall to a gully which leads to a soakaway pit filled with large stones which can be disinfected at intervals looks after the daily washing down. Today's large metal bucket of drinking water is tomorrow's washing down water. The base of the frame is *slightly* raised above the concrete on tiles or slates to allow the water to run off. A weldmesh or corrugated roof over the run stops your dog jumping out or someone else's jumping in to 'hot' bitches and a basic wooden bench above the concrete in the outside run keeps arthritis at bay.

I do not use bedding. Bedding may make *you* feel better but it does nothing for the dog. It harbours external parasites and if a dog goes to bed wet, the bedding gets wet and stays wet until changed whereas if on wood the dog soon dries out. If you insist on using bedding either shredded paper or umpteen pieces of VetBed (or similar) changed daily is probably your best bet. (On our return from hunting we used to turn wet and muddy hounds into the straw shed for ten minutes while we had a cup of tea. We would then bring out very clean, dry hounds, feed them and bed them down on fresh straw in the kennels.)

CAGES

Car cages are brilliant inventions. They can be used as whelping boxes, for immobilising an injured dog with, say, a cut pad or, if fitted with a plastic tray, for carrying deer carcasses. I have seen the value of a car or a fitted kitchen reduced by several thousand pounds in the same number of minutes by a dog that meant business! I prefer the solid sided cages such as the Lintran to the all weldmesh ones. The former are draught proof, retain most of the dirt *within* the cage and give a pup a greater feeling of security. They are probably also more expensive! Weldmesh cages can be improved by cladding them *externally* with thin plywood on light battens. If you must keep your gundog in the house I cannot recommend too strongly that you obtain a car cage large enough to contain the *adult* dog and that is the pup's home from Day 1. Raise one side very slightly so that any puppy widdle runs away from the bedding and raise the whole thing on a base several inches above the floor to avoid draughts. That is to all intents and purposes its kennel while your garden is its run. Obviously its routine must allow for *frequent* chances to 'empty' outside. When you are asleep or away from home you can rest secure in the knowledge that World War 3 will not have occurred in your absence! Rather than lugging it to and fro it eventually becomes easier to have a second cage for the car.

If, despite a secure garden, you have a 'Houdini' or a dog that tries to kill the neighbour's cat, an electric cattle fence wire on insulators either along the top of the garden fence or 6-9 in. (15-23 cm) above ground level depending on the escape route will have pretty instant results as long as the culprit is earthed when it tries to 'do a runner', so avoid plastic chain link. After a couple of days you can return the electric fencing machine to the lender but leave the wire *in situ*.

CARS

To a dog a car is merely a mobile kennel and later on the car means *fun*. Again, a car cage saves a lot of hassle, the back of an estate car or hatchback can be left open in hot weather, the dog does not slide about so much and the car interior remains relatively clean (if that is important!). With older dogs I trap the end of the lead under the tailgate which anchors the dog in the back and eventually the lead becomes unnecessary. They now make harnesses that clip into seat belts for restraining dogs in saloon cars. Initially, take the pup on short journeys for its daily scamper about and increase the distance as the pup grows older. Remember that ten miles round the lanes make for worse travelling than 100 miles on a motorway. If a youngster builds up an aversion to the car (its first three journeys are usually leaving mum and two visits to the vet!), feed it in a stationary car and eventually feed it while the engine is running – with the fumes being blown away. When you eventually get onto the serious stuff remember that no dog can operate with a nose full of car fumes – a disadvantage of some trailers. Most pups eventually grow out of salivating or being carsick if everything is done gradually and sensibly and it is not made to travel on a full stomach. (Facing backwards makes most children carsick.) From the start never let a dog leave a vehicle until commanded and always walk the dog right back to the vehicle *at heel*. These two common sense precautions may well save your pride and joy from going under the wheels of a passing juggernaut. In the light of increasing dognapping, some sort of heavy duty chain and padlock arrangement in hot weather makes sense. If your dog develops the annoying habit of standing up whenever you reverse, accelerating and then braking hard will throw it off its feet and teach it to lie down. Prevent your dog from jumping up on the sides of any vehicle – it does not earn many brownie points with car proud drivers. I have often threatened to wire my old van up to an electric fencing unit!

A good kennel and dog box/car cage (not to mention the 4 x 4!) are part and parcel of a gundog trainer's equipment and will probably cost far more than their first occupant but should last long enough to accommodate all your subsequent gundogs so get the best you can afford.

Set aside time to walk away from the vehicle for ever-increasing distances and, if the dog barks or whines, return swiftly and rattle a long stick/hosepipe at the dog in the box, saying 'QUIET' extremely sharply.

4: Choosing a Pup

Marry in haste, repent at leisure. Anon

You will have already decided upon the breed you want, what time of year to buy it and how and where you will keep it. Since you are going to have ten or more seasons work out of your dog it makes sense to do your homework rather than rushing out and buying the first pup you see in advertised in the local rag. Two things that I have already said but they bear repeating are, first, that it is difficult enough to get a good gundog that will do your job from the best sire and dam available without inviting trouble and second, that all the British breeds of gundog have two lines – Working and Show. So, for heaven's sake, if getting a British breed get a working bred pup whose pedigree will include a number of ancestors with the initials 'FTCh' (Field Trial Champion) before their name. If they have any of the dreaded 'Ch' (Champion) or 'Sh Ch' (Show Champion) then avoid them like the plague. (The only exception to this rule is the flatcoat but even they have some 'lines' [bloodlines] that are better workers than others although these are often also exhibited.) However, unless you want to run your dog in Field Trials yourself, do not buy a pup with virtually *every* ancestor a Field Trial Champion since it is likely to be either too 'hot' or oversensitive for normal shooting work. On the other hand, the continental Hunter Pointer Retrievers are currently bred for both show and work although there are moves afoot in the shooting world to bring the HPRs in line with the British gundog breeds. But as things stand now, any HPR puppy is likely to have 'FTCh' and/or 'ShCh' in its pedigree.

Word of mouth is the best way to get a pup but, failing that, the shooting periodicals particularly *Shooting Times* (weekly) and *Shooting Gazette* (monthly) carry a lot of working bred puppies. If you are a complete novice ask for a copy of the pedigree and discuss it with a *knowledgeable* gundog friend who may telephone the breeder on your behalf and *tactfully* ask a few pertinent questions. Most breeders of gundogs are pretty genuine people and only too happy that their puppies go to working homes – but they still have a litter of puppies to sell! The majority will usually be frank with you because they want the pups to be a success rather than trying to offload a litter just for the cash. The sort of questions one should tactfully ask the breeder is 'What are both parent's hip scores?' (The lower the two numbers – which refer to the x-ray of the left and right hips – the better: 0:0 is perfect and 53:53 is atrocious.) Labradors in particular have a history of hip problems but, like eye problems, not every gundog breed has every hereditary problem – some have none at all. 'Have both parents had their eyes tested?' (particularly important with Labradors and springer spaniels) 'What sort of shooting do you use the bitch for?' 'Is she easy to handle?' 'Is she a 'hard going' [energetic] type or a 'plodder'?' 'What is the bitch's mouth like on a running pheasant?' 'Is she quiet at a peg or in a pigeon/duck hide?' (Hard mouth and whining are very hereditary.) 'Why did you choose that particular sire?' 'When are the pups ready to go?' (Seven weeks old is the normal age to buy a pup.) 'How much do the pups cost?' Male pups are frequently a bit cheaper than bitch pups and state whether you want a dog or a bitch. If the answer to these questions is satisfactory arrange to go and see them. With gundogs, either puppies or trained dogs, you do *not* get what you pay for. Each breed has an 'average' price and the price asked is what the vendor thinks he or she can get for it rather than the intrinsic worth of the dog. Beware any very high or very low prices although 'unregistered' (not Kennel Club [KC] registered) pups fetch considerably less than registered ones. Perhaps unfair but that is the way it is. If you can manage it, take pound notes along rather than a cheque book.

Most breeders operate on a 'first come, first served' principle having been messed about in the past! However they should make that point clear to enquirers. (A £100 deposit will usually secure a pup if you cannot get there straight away but you may have less choice.) Wear sensible clothes and take barb'r-n-wellies since exuberant puppies usually manage to cover everyone with mud! Remember that all seven week old puppies, both good and bad, look attractive and have 'lovely temperaments' so leave any children behind to avoid moral blackmail! Be guided by gut feelings. Some set-ups/litters seem right while others do not and if you do not like a dog today, you will not like it tomorrow. The dam of the pups is usually a good indication of how they will turn out. You are unlikely to see the sire since he usually belongs to someone else. The pups should be bright eyed and bushy tailed with shiny coats although all pups 'crash' after a meal. The top and bottom sets of teeth should meet as nature intended and *firm* stools should be in evidence. If you are not happy with what you see decline politely and look elsewhere. Murphy's Law says that pups will catch fleas or a 24-hour bug the day the advertisement comes out!(I speak from experience!). However, if you are happy, carry on . . .

With some breeds colour or size may be a deciding factor whereas with, say, a litter of black Labradors you may as well shut both eyes and grab one! What is shy at seven weeks may well be bold at seven months and *vice-versa*. Taking each pup out of the run individually will give a better idea of its character than seen *en masse*.The breeder should supply you with a pedigree ('family tree') and, if you are lucky, a Kennel Club registration form (*signed on the back*) but these are notoriously long in coming through and will probably be sent on. The breeder will advise you about inoculations, worming and feeding and should give you enough food to *gradually* change over to your preferred brand. (All young animals must have *gradual* change.) Any reputable breeder has a responsibility towards what they breed and here at The Warren we always offer to have any puppy back if, for whatever reason, it cannot be kept, as long as it has not been taken shooting.

You may have already decided on a 'kennel name' (as distinct from the *official* fanciful name on the KC Registration) or one may (eventually!) suggest itself but any name should obey two rules. It should be short and sharp of either one or two syllables and it should not sound similar to a word of command. Avoid the popular names such as 'Ben', 'Sam', 'Amber', 'Meg' as every shoot or training kennel is full of 'em and do not have a similar sounding name to a dog that you already have, e.g., 'Beth' and 'Bess'. A beater I once met in Cornwall had three springers called 'One', 'Two' and 'Three' – I could not fault that one!!

If you have a car cage, fine but most pups last about 30 seconds in the average cardboard box. The passenger foot well of the car lined with plenty of newspaper is as good a place as any to transport a pup (they cannot see out and consequently have less chance of being sick – just!) and have paper kitchen towels at the ready. Do not let it out to empty or have a run on the way home – it will probably run away, get run over or catch some horrible disease. Just concentrate on getting it home in one piece and if you discover anything about which you are not happy, contact the breeder and discuss it *straight away*.

From now on you may be forgiven for wondering what you ever did with your spare time!

5: 'What goes on Between the Ears'

If you want to train a dawg, act dumb.
Delmar Smith, legendary American trainer.

This is an incredibly boring chapter, particularly for the would-be trainer who wants to get on with it. If it makes you feel any better, I hardly worked myself up into a frenzy when writing it! Unfortunately, it is compulsory reading for any novice wanting a decently trained dog because, according to all the pundits from Aristotle onwards, the whole nitty gritty of the way in which a dog's mind works, and therefore its subsequent training, is contained therein. If you cannot or will not take the trouble to 'read it, learn it and inwardly digest it' I suggest that you return this tome forthwith to the shelf! As my big game hunting chums in Africa used to say when after a specific big cat, 'When you have got into his mind, he's yours.'

Dogs, like horses, are not intelligent – thank heavens! They are basic, simple things with a basic, simple mind. If they were as intelligent as most people give them credit for, we could never train them, or, more accurately, they would never let themselves be trained! One frequently hears, 'How intelligent, he has learned how to open the back door.' Rubbish! 'Every time he jumped up at the door and caught the door lever on the way down, the door opened. Eventually the penny dropped,' would be a far more accurate way to describe this 'intelligence'.

Several points to remember which will make the eventual training of a dog easier are that we live primarily by our eyes whereas dogs live primarily by their noses, that dogs are always acutely aware of place/territory and that they appear to exist purely in the present and certainly have no conception of the future. They also have extremely sharp hearing so there is no need to bawl at a dog sitting six feet away! You will notice out shooting that the best trained dogs always have the quietest handlers.

The successful trainer is always putting his or herself in the dog's place and looking at everything from the dog's point of view. The often quoted example of the dog running off and getting a hiding when it returns sums this up. Obviously the dog thinks that it is getting a hiding for its most recent action, i.e. returning, and is even less likely to return promptly next time. A dog will always associate praise or blame with its *last* act or experience. The very successful trainer is always one jump ahead of the dog and anticipating problems before they arise. For example, the trainer sees a distant dog walker approaching with his pet running loose. Instead of waiting until his pupil also sees the other dog and rushes off to join it while ignoring the recall whistle, the switched-on trainer quietly slips the lead on his pupil and walks him off in the other direction, thereby avoiding a confrontation. As a puppy grows up life is a series of 'experiences' some of which have pleasant associations, some unpleasant ones and some merely neutral. It is up to the trainer to capitalise on this basic fact. When it hears a feed bowl rattled, food is likely to appear or if it growls at the cat, its nose is scratched etc., etc. Later on, when its haunches are gently pushed down accompanied by the quiet request to 'SIT' and its ears are fondled, life is pleasant. If it subsequently tries to move, it is growled at with the harsh command 'SIT' and its haunches are pushed sharply down, life thus becoming unpleasant. It is simply 'trigger' and 'association' as so completely demonstrated by Pavlov. With gundog training the command is the trigger and the association is the action that the dog has been taught to associate with the trigger and I stress '*taught*' - there is a popular misconception among many dog owners that dogs thoroughly understand the whole of the English language (four letter words included!). So 'SIT', a 'peep' on the whistle, a raised hand and a stamped foot will all eventually come to mean 'Sit down pretty d—mn quickly and don't even dream about moving until I say otherwise'!

In the wild, any pack of canines has the pack leader who is the dominant male (although the pack is invariably led by the dominant female). He is right at the top of the pyramid and his word is law while the baby puppies are at the bottom of the pile. All the other pack members have sorted out a pecking order among themselves between the puppies and the pack leader. As young animals get older this order can change either merely from a difference in attitude/body language or, occasionally, the mother and father of a scrap! Anyone who has had the privilege of working with a pack of hounds will be continually aware of this ongoing process. When you, the would-be trainer, takes on a young gundog it is looking for that leadership. It is up to you to provide it and the pup is conditioned from birth to accept it. However, that leadership *is not an automatic God-given right*. It has to be earned by gaining the dog's respect. Think back to your schooldays. One teacher would say 'Sit down and be quiet' and you would all be as good as gold. Another teacher would say 'Sit down and be quiet' and all hell would break loose! It was all about *respect* and the teacher consistently drawing the line at the same place. So it is with dog trainers. Psycho-whatnots apparently tell us that we humans are divided into super-dominant, normal dominant and sub-dominant in our relationships with one another. So with our relationships with our dogs but, just to complicate life, dogs also fall into three categories - strong willed, normal and submissive. Unfortunately, matching the right pup to the right owner is frequently something of a lottery. However, enough of all that old psycho stuff . . .

Training a dog is like building a house, each lesson is like a course of bricks with each course depending on the course below it being soundly built. Each lesson is based upon the previous lesson which has to be thoroughly taken on board before proceeding. For instance, lesson 1 is teaching the dog to sit at the trainer's feet, lesson 2 is to sit while the trainer walks away and lesson 3 is to sit at a distance. Obviously the dog cannot learn to sit at a distance until it has been taught to sit at the trainer's feet. To revert to the building analogy, 'No foundations – house falls down'! You skimp these basic lessons at your peril and it is essential that the basic lessons of SIT, HEEL and TURN are 110% learned and thoroughly and indelibly imprinted on your pupil's mind before going on to the more interesting stuff.

There are two basic rules for training *any* dog to do *any*thing and once you have taken these on board, the rest sorts itself out:

1 *Life to a dog is either black or white. There are no shades of grey. If it does well you praise it and if it does wrong you 'rollick' it.* (And I mean black or white - not dark grey or light grey.)
2 *A dog is being consistently trained 24 hours a day.*

By the second rule I mean that there is no point in giving your hound half an hour's square bashing every evening and letting it do whatever it likes for the other 23½ hours. By consistently, I mean that the dog is *always* allowed on the car seat or *never* allowed on the car seat. You cannot say one day, 'You have clean paws today, Fido. Sit on the seat' and the next day, 'You have dirty paws, Fido. Stay on the floor.' Dogs do not 'think' like that. Either Fido is always allowed on the seat or never allowed on it. Similarly, either the dog always sits when you tell it or never sits when you tell it. Dog training is about *always* and *never*. It is not about 'sometimes' or 'occasionally' or 'if I can be bothered' or 'if Fido feels like it.' Conversely, never give any dog any order that you are not in a position to enforce or you are merely teaching it to *disobey* a command. That is how they become lager louts.

It is extremely easy to become too psychological about training dogs which usually means that you have erred in crediting them with human-type intelligence. We have all done it and have got ourselves into deep water. However, as soon as one gets back to basics and keeps things simple these problems sort themselves out and the poor confused dog knows where it stands again. Now let us get back to practicalities.

6: The Formative Months

When The Good Lord made time, he made plenty of it. Irish saying.

Rather like Shakespeare's 'The Seven Ages of Man', a working gundog goes through a number of different stages or periods in its life which are fluid and flow from one to the next:

Up to seven weeks	Baby puppy/whelp
7 weeks to 7 months	Puppy
7 months to 9-10 months	Young dog (spaniels usually start training at 7 months)
7-10 months to 11-16 months	In training (age depending on breed. 4-6 months trg.)
11-16 months to 24-30 months	Post-training but still very much learning
30 months to c 10 years	Working
10 years plus	Semi-retired or retired

Most working dogs are either made or broken between seven weeks and seven months old. These formative months are invariably a delicate balance between allowing a growing pup to do its own thing, gain experience of the big wide world, develop its latent hunting and retrieving instincts and generally grow up and become more mature on the one hand, while maintaining control and good manners without unduly inhibiting the pup on the other. It is a balancing act requiring common sense and a certain amount of gut feeling. I wish I had a pound for every pup I knew of that was a cuddly bundle of much adored fluff that suddenly grew up and became a raving lager lout overnight because no-one had instilled any basic domestic manners into it from the start. If ever a youngster defies you to take something from it, turf it off some furniture or to leave a particular place then *go for it straightaway with all guns blazing* and make it wish that the idea had never even occurred to it. On the training side one should also prevent any major gundog vices from becoming ingrained because the more any habit, good or bad, becomes ingrained, the more difficult it is to eradicate. If bad habits can be 'nipped in the bud' before they become established life becomes so much easier. (I recently had to re-train a young Labrador bitch that someone else had made an excellent job of teaching to walk to heel on the *left*. A left-handed gun had bought her part-trained and I had to teach her to walk on the *right*. The left habit had become well ingrained.)

Never forget that *Field Trials are won in kennels*. A happy, well fed, healthy, confident but obedient dog that knows what is expected of it is halfway there.

It is extremely important to establish a *regular* kennel routine right from day one. Then the pup knows exactly where it is and that gives it terrific confidence. When the trainer opens the kennel door and says 'GET ON' the pup runs out because it wants to go and play. When he puts the food bowl inside the kennel and says 'KENNEL' the pup runs in because it wants to eat etc., etc. By associating the pup's natural desires with a simultaneous relevant command that pup grows up obeying the trainer's every command without actually realising it. When one eventually comes on to serious training the job is already half done because that pup is already conditioned to do whatever the trainer says. (Never let a dog that is barking out of its kennel or it will 'think' that if it barks long enough it will be let out or that being let out is a reward for barking.) Apart from the regular kennel routine *let the puppy be a puppy* and a happy puppy at that. Trying to put an old head on young shoulders is a sure road to ruin. *The greatest single problem of the one-puppy-owner or the single-dog-trainer is to accept that the best course of action during this stage is mainly to do nothing!* At the puppy stage the pup should be a puppy, a glorified family pet getting loads of tender loving care from the family, enjoying life, beating up the happy home (plus the nearby environment), going shopping, supporting the local football team, giving the locals a hard time and generally growing up. Do not be tempted to enrol your puppy in the usual 30-hooligans-in-the-village-hall obedience classes. It will do a future working gundog nothing but harm. Never lose sight of the fact that, with working dogs, obedience is purely a means to an end and is never an end in itself. Local weekly *gundog* training classes for the breeds similar to your own are a different thing altogether and, if nothing else, will get your pup used to mixing with other dogs and you will meet other gundog people which whom to discuss problems. Other trainers prefer to plough their own furrow. Every novice trainer (and the average gundog owner has a new pup every ten years) has read all the books, seen all the videos, worn all the Tee-shirts and cannot wait to thrust all their knowledge upon this seven-week-old bundle of fluff. The fact that they did not let their kids sit their GCSEs until they were 15 years old is irrelevant. '*Thou shalt be an instant gundog.*' Balderdash! Far more gundogs are ruined from being *overtrained* than *undertrained.*

FEEDING

At the risk of stating the obvious, if a dog is too fat you are feeding it too much and if too thin you are not feeding it enough as long as the internal parasites (worms to you and me) are under control. Too much weight puts an unnecessary strain on the heart and young limbs and you will see far more fat dogs at the vets than thin ones! A seven-week-old puppy needs four meals a day, either two of milk and puppy meal and two of meat given alternately, or four feeds of a complete puppy meal. It is extremely easy to make a puppy faddy – like children, they will be if you let them! Put their food down and after ten minutes harden your heart and remove it. No healthy dog will starve itself and they will soon get the message. If you have more than one dog feed them separately or you will end up with one fat one and one thin one! Contrary to popular opinion not all gundogs are make pigs of themselves even with competition and my line of spaniels are all very shy feeders. There are many excellent makes of complete dog food on the market catering for all canine workloads from the family pet to racing greyhounds and for all stages in a dog's life It makes sense to get whichever one is available locally at your pet shop or farm co-op. A 20 kg bag will last the average adult gundog from four to eight weeks so they are also economical. The manufacturer's guide to amounts of food is only a guide and should be coupled with common sense. Like people, some dogs get fat on very little food whereas others seem to stay thin however much they eat. More and more gundogs appear to be allergic to wheat gluten which *may* be why your dog has loose stools and is not thriving as it should but many firms now manufacture gluten free complete dog foods. Always make all changes in a dog's food *gradually* so beg a couple of days supply of puppy food from the breeder when you take the puppy home. At twelve to sixteen weeks the feeds can be reduced to three daily but increase the amount and at about six months plus it can be weaned onto the adult version. By seven to nine months the feeds can again be reduced to two a day. Although many adult gundogs are only fed once a day I have found that most gundogs assimilate two smaller feeds a day better than one large one. I therefore feed one-third in the morning and two-thirds in the evening throughout a dog's life. Remember that in winter when it is working a dog may need half as much food again and in very hot weather they need very little and a dog kept in a warm house in winter will again require less than a dog kennelled outside.

Puppy food should contain no more that 21-24 % protein while 18-20% is plenty for an adult dog. Beware using excessive protein diets. It not only eventually blows their kidneys but also hypes up their minds like a racehorse on oats. I find that some of the hyperactive nutters (who have frequent fits) that come in for training have been fed on protein levels designed for partridge chicks! When I drop them down to about 18% they revert to being a normal dog. A dog's stomach is designed by nature, like all carnivores, to operate on a 'gorge and starve' principle. I therefore have great reservations about the modern concentrated feeds that claim an egg cup full daily is sufficient and I certainly have great reservations about so called 'scientific' diets available only from limited outlets. Although I have always been a great fan of raw tripe and raw meat it is not without problems in terms of regular availability, time spent in getting and preparing it and the general muck and smell, particularly in the summer. However tins of dog meat (90+% water) and biscuit are, in my opinion, a complete waste of time and money. Ox shin bones are great for any dog but will cause aggro if you have more than one dog. *Sensible* household scraps can *replace* some of the complete dog food.

Do not worry if it is not you that actually feeds the pup or young dog. A dog's allegiance is always to that person who gives it its free running exercise and, later on, its work.

PARASITES

All dogs carry worms and in times of stress such as changing homes, illness, a hard week of concentrated work, etc., these will multiply. Puppies need treating for roundworms at three to four weekly intervals up to six months and thereafter for tapeworms every six months. The beginning and end of the shooting season is as good a time as any. However it is a myth that only young puppies get roundworms and only older dogs get tapeworms. I have found tapeworms in eight-week-old puppies and I treat most of my adult 'English' pointers for roundworms twice a year – sometimes with eye-opening results! Get your worming tablets from your veterinary surgeon rather than the chemist or pet shop although I, personally, have not found the new 'multi-spectrum' wormers to be very effective. These days you will not always see the results on the kennel floor. Since Alugan was taken off the market, the control of external parasites such as fleas, lice and ticks has become a lot more difficult (and expensive). If a dog is continually scratching and biting at its coat have a thorough look (with a magnifying glass if necessary) and then discuss the best way of ridding your dog of 'passengers' with your vet. New products are being brought out all the time. There is no stigma attached in a dog getting parasites but only in the owner not getting rid of them!

EXERCISE

There is a great difference between 'taking a dog for a walk' and 'controlled exercise'. Allowing young dogs to charge about out of control merely risks malforming young limbs, causing unnecessary hip dysplasia and it eventually gets them fitter and fitter until they end up like a high performance car with the throttle jammed open and no brakes and steering because no-one has ever taught them anything! Once you have started to seriously train a pup, a walk can do nothing but harm. Either it walks to heel on a lead (which is probably all right for deer dogs and covert shooting dogs) but this gives them little actual exercise and only serves to inhibit a hunting breed from getting out and actually hunting or, if off the lead, it is charging about out of control, probably chasing game and generally amusing itself at your expense. One step forward on the training area then becomes two steps backwards on the walk. Forget it. Pups need a 10 minute scamper in a controlled area (the garden) several times a day which can gradually be increased to 20 minutes in a nearby field as the pup gets older. Hunting breeds can be taken to 'interesting', i.e. slightly 'gamey', areas and allowed to run about and investigate under close supervision. This is how they teach themselves about wind and scent and going into cover. My pointing breed pups wear a whippet collar trailing a 9-12 ft (3-4 m) length of nylon rope with the end burned off. If they come on point I surreptitiously pick up the end of the line and I have all the advantages of the point with none of the disadvantages of diving in early to flush and/or chasing the departing quarry. Trailing a line later on also inhibits the potential hooligan for at the back of its minds always lurks the possibility that you can grab hold of the end of the line and give it a sharp jerk even if they are, in reality, too far away for this to actually happen.

Long before I take a pup out for the first time I decide how many yards away from me (depending on the breed and its eventual job) I want that pup to 'quarter' ['zig-zag' while hunting] – say 10 yards either side. I have an imaginary semi-circle with a 10 yard radius in front of me and every time that pup reaches the edge of that semicircle I give a 'PIP PIP' on my whistle and go in the opposite direction. The pup follows me naturally and has a fuss made of it and thus learns to turn on the whistle without really being aware of it. If the pup gets a bit independent I hide behind a tree or lie down out of sight in cover and the pup soon comes looking for me. Should that pup eventually look at me when I blow the turn whistle and then give me 'two fingers' and carry on doing as it pleases (as any pup worth its salt will do sooner or later) *I do not* keep blowing the turn whistle hoping that it will eventually turn: I *run* across to that pup, pick it up by the scruff of the neck without saying a thing, I return to the exact spot where it actually disobeyed the command. I then shake it by the jowls (commensurate with its size and temperament) and glare into its eyes while repeating that 'PIP PIP' on the whistle several times over. Having done that I let it hunt on again and the *next* time I give the 'PIP PIP' that pup will invariably turn sharply towards me. I then make an extra special fuss of it thus demonstrating black/white, good/bad. I seldom have to do this more than once or twice during that pup's life and none of this is actually *teaching* the pup anything but merely conditioning it for later on.

On these jaunts I encourage pups to explore bracken, long grass, rushes and other 'soft' cover by walking through it, tossing the odd ball into it, hiding in it and calling the pup to me and generally getting them to *enjoy* cover. At this stage I avoid brambles, nettles, whins/gorse, blackthorn or any 'hard' cover that would hurt a pup and thus put it off. That can come much later when the pup is ready for it, i.e., goes in naturally. From time to time call the pup over, slip on a hitherto hidden lead and make a fuss of it sof 10-20 seconds before releasing it again. It does not then associate being called with return to barracks.

I have repeatedly stressed that one should refrain from trying to train a pup until it is old enough to take serious training. If one dare generalise, the *optimum* ages for the different breeds are as follows, but they may be far too early for a shy, sensitive bitch or far too late for a boisterous hooligan of a dog. I *generally* start spaniels at 6-8 months, retrievers at 8-11 months and pointing breeds at 10-15 months. As I said earlier, one should buy ones pup so that it is at this age in the beginning of the summer. However, there are a number of important lessons that are best taught much earlier in life because the pup is more receptive then. Some of these are swimming, respect for sheep and other livestock, getting into cover, blood trailing for deer dogs, 'HEEL' for deer dogs and 'non-slip retrievers' which is a quaint term for what are now more prosaically called 'peg dogs'.

SWIMMING

Every breed of dog can be taught to swim but some breeds are better natural swimmers than others. Whether 'English' pointers and setters need to be taught at all is a moot point but mine certainly enjoy a swim in a lochan during a hot day on the hill. The younger the pup, the greater the confidence (like kids on ponies) and persuading little pups to follow you through shallow streams in warm weather builds up this confidence. The best tutor is the pup's mother or another dog that will give it a gentle lead without half drowning the poor little devil. Although no gundog can be said to be a competent swimmer until it can deal with flowing water or even the sea, start in still water. Wait for a hot day and be prepared to get wet! If a pup already retrieves a dummy the lesson can be learnt much easier. Otherwise it is the wellies or, better still, the waders technique. Throw a tennis ball *along* the edge of a pond with gently sloping banks to land in the water just off shore and upwind of the pup By throwing it some 15 yards more or less parallel to the shoreline the pupil will get up a fair head of steam before reaching the area of the floating ball. Command 'HI LOST' and then *keep quiet* and let the pup concentrate on literally taking the plunge. Do not try and 'steady' it [make it wait before sending it] which only gives it time to decide whether it wants to go in or not but let it 'run in' [retrieve straight away]. When it retrieves the ball crouch down on the shore and intercept the retrieve. Make a big fuss of the pup. Continue to throw the ball just a bit further from the shore every time but remember that swimming is very tiring for a puppy. (For some reason dogs will often retrieve an object from water that they will not pick on land – worth bearing in mind for possible retrieving problems later on.) Thereafter use every hot weather opportunity to ensure that it really enjoys swimming. When I have taken the ball from the pup and it naturally shakes the water from its coat I command 'SHAKE' in a cart-before-the-horse situation. One can gradually increase the distance from the shore before commanding 'SHAKE' which eventually gives you time to stand at right angles to avoid a cold shower and prevents the dog gripping the retrieve *too firmly* to prevent it from flying out of its mouth while shaking, or putting down the retrieve to shake which means that a wounded duck will dive into the reeds to probably never be seen again.

If you have a reluctant swimmer wait for a hot day. Don wellies or waders and walk into the pond with the pup cradled in your arms. Gently lower it into the water until its natural buoyancy takes over and then gently withdraw your arms. The pup will invariably swim to the bank. (This method is not to be confused with literally 'chucking it in at the deep end' which invariably causes more problems than it solves.) Repeat the lesson tactfully until the pup gains confidence when you can probably call it out to you. Once it realises that there is nothing to fear and, indeed, swimming is great fun you are away. One winter I had a particularly obtuse golden retriever that (unusually for 'goldens') loathed water but the owner was particularly keen on wildfowling. Eventually, near to losing my cool, I put the slip lead on, ordered 'HEEL' and walked into the training pond nearly up to my waist in some *extremely* cold water. The dog's feet came off the bottom and we did a circuit or two of the pond with the dog swimming at heel and me freezing my whatnots off. I loosed the slip lead and off she went having the time of her life and never looked back. She became a fine wildfowling bitch thereafter – but I cannot recommend the method! (I eventually discovered that she had slipped over a weir as a pup . . .!)

Most gundog books tell you how to teach a dog to swim but few teach you how to *stop* them from swimming! I teach waterholics to *leave* the water by attaching a long nylon line to a collar, allowing them to swim in a snag-free pond, giving the recall whistle and then towing them firmly ashore. On a South American cattle ranch I also learned to be a dab hand with a lassoo! Once a dog enjoys swimming I always 'drop' them [make them sit or lie down] on approaching water and then send them in on command or vary the lesson by walking them to heel *away* from the water because waterholics can be a real nuisance at times.

SHEEP

Speaking as a sheep farmer myself who has seen a dozen or more ewes with their throats torn out and their entrails and embryo lambs strewn around the field by a dog that 'only wanted to play', I need hardly stress the importance of having ones dogs entirely safe with livestock. I make no apology for saying that it is one lesson where, if needs be, I will be as hard on a dog as is necessary. One cannot go through life avoiding livestock 'in case my dog chases them'. Equally, any dog that is not safe with stock will eventually lose you and possibly your friends your shooting/training ground, cost you a lot of money and end up with the dog being shot dead by an irate but fully justified farmer. Far better to face the problem head on with a five minute lesson while the pup is at an impressionable age and get it over and done with for the rest of that dogs life. Some dogs show no apparent desire to chase sheep or other stock but, in most cases, I believe that the instinct to do so is always lying dormant in any dog since sheep, like hares and deer, are a natural quarry species for a dog. I therefore give every dog through my hands the same short, sharp lesson.

The method I use was shown to me some years ago by my friend and mentor, Bryan Gough of the Shamdale affix. I approach a flock of sheep from down wind with the dog on a slip lead and a bamboo cane or 3 ft (1 m) length of alkathene water pipe hidden down my wellie. At the exact moment that the sheep

Make your dog feel part of the team – the third leg of the stool is the photographer! Hungarian Vizsla with Harris hawk on a rabbit.

PLATE 5

Teaching a Bavarian Mountain Bloodhound to follow a blood trail.

A convenient way to stalk with an unruly small dog, in this case a Teckel.

PLATE 6

(below)
Bob White quail may be kept in the garage. The re-entry funnel was padded for the photograph.

run away I catch the pup unawares with a sharp cut across the fleshy part of its quarters snarling 'SHEEP'. The dog 'thinks' to itself 'every time those things run away I get a pain in the backside'. I repeat the lesson once or twice more and as soon as the pup hangs back on approaching the sheep I remove the lead and walk close to the sheep saying nothing. The pupil will generally give them a wide berth. If any owner cannot bring him or herself to teach this lesson in a businesslike way I, personally, would seriously doubt their suitability to train a gundog.

The fact that that pup is all right with *those* sheep in *that* particular field is not a cast iron guarantee at this stage that it is all right with every flock in every field so some reinforcement elsewhere may be necessary. *Do not* imagine that because your dog is safe with sheep in 'in-bye' [grass] fields, it is automatically safe with sheep on moorland. *It is not*. Hill sheep, particularly heather-fed hill sheep, are, to a dog, a completely different animal. They appear to smell more like a deer and the same lesson must be taught with hill sheep on 'the hill'. Baby lambs, particularly when temporarily away from the ewe, seem to exert a strange fascination for a dog, so be on your guard.

Several points to remember : a dog that has spent some time in a car or kennel and is 'fresh' is more likely to be 'sheepy' than one that has run for twenty minutes; more than one dog is a pack and two dogs will egg one another on and, again, are more likely to chase sheep; any dog that has pulled down a sheep *and tasted blood* can never really be trusted again and should be under particularly close supervision and 'sheepiness' is, to an extent, hereditary. If your dog has not been in contact with sheep for some time, a cautionary growl of 'SHEEP' on first encountering them again should serve to remind it.

Always walk any dog, however safe, through other people's sheep *on a lead* as a matter of courtesy and should any dog ever 'take a dive at' some sheep, take action immediately and let justice be seen to be done because that is the time when someone is bound to be watching!

The same lesson applies equally to poultry, cattle and loose or ridden horses although my children's unshod Shetland pony was a bit 'free' with her heels and great for teaching pups to respect equines!

DEER, HARES AND CATS

All these are also natural canine prey species and, if unchecked, most dogs will chase them. Because of the history of feral cats on the continent most HPRs will kill a cat as soon as look at it and this does little to improve relations with the neighbours! Nothing is more infuriating, apart from being bad training, than having ones dog taking off after deer and/or hares and it is a habit which, once ingrained, is almost impossible to break. Use the methods just described for sheep chasing and if it causes ones dog to 'blink' [pretend that they are not there] hares or not to retrieve them then so be it, but that is the lesser of the two evils. Once a dog is steady to hares it can usually be persuaded to retrieve them when into its second shooting season. 'Deer aversion therapy' is best taught in a deer park or on a deer farm. No dog destined for deer work should ever be allowed to chase (unshot) deer more than once. Thereafter keep it on a lead. Sheep killers frequently make excellent deer dogs when their aptitude can be harnessed to following up wounded deer.

I detest the idea of 'electric collars' with a deep loathing but, since they were originally developed to teach dogs to respect/avoid rattlesnakes and alligators in the USA, I can accept the principle that they might have a use either where a particular form of 'riot' [forbidden quarry] could not be encountered as a puppy or in training (we have virtually no deer or hares in Breconshire), or where the trainer is no longer sufficiently agile enough (for whatever reason) to 'explain to the dog the error of its ways'.

POULTRY

No gundog should obviously kill poultry but a certain amount of tact should be used, particularly with brown-coloured hens.

So to reiterate, be in no hurry to start actually training your pup during these formative months but concentrate on bringing up a well-balanced citizen without stifling any of the right instincts and it will be time well spent in doing nothing!

Having sorted out all the above factors just let it be a puppy. (As I write my young son is rolling on the kitchen floor with a six-month-old Labrador puppy working out which will be the eventual possessor of a beach ball - all good harmless stuff and great for both of them.)

7: Basic Training - 'The Rock upon which it is all built'

Make haste slowly. Anon

Deciding when a dog is ready to start serious training is akin to the advice given on combining malting barley – 'When you think it is ready, take a holiday and then start on it when you return'! In both cases one is tempted to start rather earlier than one probably should. I make no apology for repeating that the basic training is the foundation upon which all subsequent training is based and should be 110% sound before even dreaming of going on to 'the more interesting stuff' and *you skimp it at your peril.* Nearly all the so-called badly trained dogs out shooting were never badly trained at all, just insufficiently trained. It is not called 'Basic Training' for nothing! When I have a client's dog here for training, at least half of the 16-20 weeks is spent on the training field instilling the, to some, boring and mundane lessons of SIT, STAY, HEEL, HERE, TURN and basic RETRIEVING until that dog is virtually brainwashed to SIT or TURN at the touch of a whistle. Only then do I think about progressing further. I consider that it is always dangerous to give a time scale. It takes as long as it takes. There is no hurry. The dog will be ready when it is ready. Some children learn to read and write before others but one hopes that most of them can by the time they leave school! If a dog is not ready by the beginning of the season, so what? Since you will have ten or more seasons work out of it, why spoil it for the sake of a few weeks or even months? The old trainer's adage of 'Quick to train is quick to spoil' is a great truism and most of the 'instant wonders' I encounter that are turning somersaults through paper hoops at six months old are three-parts ruined by twelve months old.

WORDS OF COMMAND

Most gundog words of command are in pretty general use and have stood the test of time. In many cases there are recognised alternatives. It does not matter a jot which one you use or whether you make up your own *as long as you ALWAYS use the same ones*. If you are working more than one dog continue to use exactly the same commands but prefix them by that dog's name if you wish. However, with experience, they soon learn which dog you are addressing. You can get into the devil of a muddle in a hot spot using different commands and whistles for different dogs! (On a young dog's first day in the beating line, a dozen handlers are all using identical whistles simultaneously but the pup soon recognises its handler's way of blowing his.) Here are the most common words of command:

SIT / HUP (a corruption of 'Hold Up' from muzzle loading days) *To sit*
DOWN *To lie down (usually pointing breeds and deer dogs only)*
HERE / COME
HEEL
GET ON / CAST ON / (GO) SEEK *To hunt*
GO PLAY *At Ease. Amuse yourself but keep out of mischief.*
GET IN *To investigate a particular bit of cover.*
CAR / HUP (assuming you use SIT!) *Get into car.*
OVER / HUP (assuming you use SIT!) *Get over, under or through an obstacle*
KENNEL / BED / BASKET *Go in/to your sleeping place.*
BACK / STAY *Remain in car or behind kennel door.*
HI LOST / FETCH *Retrieve*
DEAD / GIVE *Give up retrieve to handler.*
QUIET (Shut Up sounds too like HUP) Plus the all important 'NO'.

Any verbal or whistle command should be given authoritatively in the confident expectation that the dog will certainly obey it – when it invariably will. If you give a half-hearted command wondering whether the dog will or will not obey it then it almost certainly will not. As the horsemen say, 'Confidence travels down the reins.' There is no need to bawl out every command like a drill sergeant. Dogs have extremely good hearing but it is not uncommon to come across the 'trainer' who always bellows at his dog even if only a few yards away rather like my Indian Army grandfather who firmly believed that if one shouted at a foreigner long enough and loudly enough in English he would eventually understand you! Remember it is not only *what* you say but also *how* you say it that is important. One can use a 'cutchy coo' voice when giving a command to denote pleasure or growl the same command to express displeasure. People with a naturally gruff voice do not always realise the effect it has on a sensitive dog when they *think* they are praising it. Never forget that, except for 'once only' commands like 'FETCH', 'OVER' etc., there is no such thing as an open ended command. If given a command, e.g. SIT, that dog remains sitting until given a counter-command i.e. HERE, HEEL, HI LOST etc. In other words *you* decide when that dog should finish sitting rather than allowing the dog to decide for itself. Sounds obvious but just watch all your chums' dogs! What one is trying to achieve with SIT and HEEL is *not* a dog that is a coiled up spring ready to explode into action at the merest hint of a signal or command but a dog with a relaxed attitude of mind that is complete switched off and says to itself, 'I am quite happy to sit here/walk to heel, despite any distractions, until the cows come home or until The Boss wants me to do something else.' Until you have achieved that state of mind in your pupil do not try to progress any further. SIT and HEEL are the two lessons with which you can legitimately bore the dog to tears until it becomes second nature.

An apparently disobedient dog is often merely a confused dog simply because the trainer has just not made things clear to it. A dog should *only* hear the words of command apart from the odd praise or rollicking. For instance, 'SIT', dummy lands 'FETCH', dummy is brought back 'DEAD'. But how often does one hear 'SIT. DONT YOU DARE MOVE. HI LOST. FETCH. IT. ITS OVER THERE. WELL DONE. NOW BRING IT BACK TO ME. STOP RUNNING ROUND IN CIRCLES. BRING IT HERE. DEAD. GIVE IT TO ME.' All very confusing – especially for the poor dog.

EQUIPMENT

The amount of training equipment required to train a gundog is minimal and many a good dog has been trained with a length of baler twine, a rabbit skin dummy and a good set of teeth (which excludes the author) through which to whistle! There is now a bewildering array of tailor-made training equipment on the market and £20 should set any novice trainer up. The first requirement is a slip lead. This is an all-in-one collar and lead combined with a metal ring through which the noose should slide easily like a lasso and a sliding 'stop' which will stop the dog from literally walking out of it. Once leather, now they are universally made of nylon. The thickness is important and it should be not be much more than 3/8 in. (1 cm) thick. The 'ship's hawser' type are far too thick. White is the best colour since it can be found when dropped in the grass which olive green or black ones cannot. Psychedelic colours do not really have a place with the serious trainer. Choke chains, separate collars and leads, chain leads, extending leads and anything that does not resemble a slip lead are of *no* training value at all and can only hinder one's attempts.

A whistle on a lanyard is the next requirement. Most dogs respond better to a whistle than the human voice, a whistle disturbs game less and a whistle disguises the trainer's emotions. Staghorn and buffalo horn are fine until you lose one because no two have the same note which makes duplicating them difficult and I, personally, have never been able to get on with the 'silent' whistles. A plastic Acme 210½ answers every requirement and every 210½ sounds identical. Because they are working several hundred yards away I turn my 'English' pointers with a shepherd's whistle (a circle of tin bent in half with a hole through both halves) and I stop them with a metal Acme Thunderer referee's whistle, but for the other breeds a 210½ is more than sufficient for both stopping and turning a dog. There is no 'magic' whistle – the magic comes from the person using it! The lanyard can be as simple or elaborate as you like as long as it will not easily break. If your dog is destined to go anywhere near a driven shoot do *not* teach it to stop on a 'referee's' whistle as many keepers start and finish a drive with one. More than once I have refrained from shooting some very sporting pheasants during a drive because some clown in the beating line has been trying to stop his errant hound with a Thunderer!

An unimaginative selection of dummies is the cause of a lot of problems and the trainer with only one dummy will always have an unsteady dog because that dog will eventually learn that sooner or later it will always be asked to retrieve it. Our own idleness has made it all too easy for us to buy a selection of the ubiquitous canvas dummies. They have some advantages. They float, they can be easily thrown and they are convenient. They also have a lot of disadvantages. They are fine for a 'retrieverholic' but for an 'iffy' retriever they are about as exciting as a loaf of stale bread would be to us. Prior to canvas dummies we all made our own out of air-dried rabbit skins wrapped round a log of wood, pheasant wings glued to bits of rolled up carpet, old car radiator hoses, old lorry rope, etc., etc., and these lived in our game bags with dead rabbits and pigeons and were *interesting* items for a young dog to retrieve. Most retrieving problems were then entirely down to us, the trainers!

A starting pistol and some boxes of .22 blank ammunition only cost a few pounds and are a great aid for hunting and pointing dogs, although they are obviously unnecessary for dogs used solely for falconry as are dummy launchers and shotguns. I use the long dummy launcher blanks in my starting pistol since the short blanks are extremely fiddly especially in cold weather. (No Firearms Certificate or home security is required for the pistol.) A 15 ft (5 m) training line of nylon rope with a spring clip spliced on and a leather collar are a must for the pointing breeds.

Dummy launchers and dummies for the launcher (canvas covered ones are best) may be seen as a necessity, a luxury, a mixed blessing or an invention of the devil and will be discussed later.

A shotgun should really be used in the final stages of training although many people prefer for a number of reasons to manage without one. I train with a 20-bore which is lighter to carry, makes less noise for a young dog to cope with and makes less mess of rabbits or other game shot at close quarters but I shoot on 'serious' occasions with a 12-bore on the basis of 'the bigger blanket of "muck" I put up, the more likely something is to fly into it'!

THE TRAINING AREA

In an ideal world the training area should be a secluded, well-fenced field with some long grass or light cover, no human or animal distractions, free of game scent, reasonably sheltered and not too far from home. Later on some imagination is called for – for more realistic training areas and ones likely to hold a bit of game such as disused railway lines, industrial waste grounds, shelter belts, 'set aside' and small areas of woodland, but initially the training field is sufficient. It is extremely important that the training area is a *different* place from the exercise area. Because of the highly developed territorial instinct in any dog, it is important for it to realise the difference between the place where it plays and the place where it works and any trainer failing to realise this basic tenet will create a lot of problems for young pupils. If you try to use the same place for both jobs you will end up with a thoroughly confused dog. In the worst instance two different sides of the same field will have to suffice. Indeed, should one have to give the dog a hard time for some misdemeanour it will be unhappy on that training area for some days and one may well have to train it elsewhere until it has got over it.

PREPARATION

Before teaching any lesson at any stage of training the trainer should be positive and know exactly what he or she is going to teach the dog and how it will be taught because if the trainer is wandering about in the dark what chance has the poor dog got? The trainer will also have thought back to the last lesson, how it went, whether more of the same is needed or is it time to progress a shade further and, if so, how. Is the weather suitable? A pointing dog must have a breeze into which to hunt and it certainly helps spaniels as well. (Last autumn and winter it was either as still as the grave or blowing a howling gale - very difficult for a youngster.) If it is very hot just take it swimming. Hot, muggy days or cold, wet muddy dummies are enough to put any pup off retrieving. If it is very wet or very cold forget all about training since neither of you is likely to enjoy it. There is a great myth that every dog *must* be trained every day – rubbish! As long as the dog is kennelled between training sessions and not allowed to get up to mischief it will forget nothing and many dogs get bored with a daily square bashing. Going for a controlled 'jolly' once a week keeps them sweet. Training young bitches in season is nothing but a complete waste of time. Leave them in purdah for three weeks and do not expect them to come straight out after 21 days as though nothing had happened.

Have you got all your props to hand before you start? Nothing upsets a training period more than having to go back home for a whistle, dummy or whatever. If anything needs setting up beforehand, do it while the dog is in the car or kennel because no pupil should be left to its own devices while you concentrate on something else. Are you yourself in the right frame of mind or did you get out of bed the wrong side, get an Income Tax Demand in the post or have a row with someone? If you are out of sorts cancel the lesson or you will invariably do more harm than good. There is an old hunting saying, 'If you lose your temper, you lose your fox' for hounds can be as easily upset as gundogs. Training should be *fun* for both of you.

You will obviously know your pup's temperament by this time and a rowdy hooligan will naturally require more positive training and handling than a shy, sensitive one that has to be kidded along almost without realising that it is being trained and there will be plenty in between. Each dog will need to be treated differently according to its temperament. Dogs that have a very tough temperament are usually very positive in their work whereas dogs that have soft temperament are usually equally 'soft' in their work. What we would all dearly like is one with a soft temperament but with a very positive attitude to the job in hand but unfortunately these are extremely rare. In the early stages of training you may well find with a tough dog that it is very much a question of

'You versus the Dog'. Eventually (and this may well take weeks or even months of virtual confrontation) the dog 'says', 'OK Boss. You win. Let's do it your way now' and suddenly it becomes 'You with the Dog' which is a very sweet feeling indeed.

THE DROP

This is the first lesson that any gundog is taught and the old adage of 'A spaniel that will stop is a spaniel half trained' still holds good. This is the first time that you impose your complete authority upon that dog and actually *teach* it to obey a specific command and your success or otherwise will set the whole tone for its future education. The 'drop' (or SIT) is the kingpin upon which all other training is based. The twin objectives are for the pupil to ultimately sit as quickly as possible and for as long as necessary. It may seem a paradox but it is invariably true. At the Swedish Wildlife Management College I understand that each pupil has his own dog which lives with him rather like police dogs do here. After a few weeks the students and their charges all go to a public café in the mountains, sit their dogs outside and go in for lunch while the public inevitably make a fuss of the dogs outside. When the students emerge an hour later if any dog has moved both handler and pupil have failed. *That* is sitting!

When you get to the training field remove the slip lead and command 'GO PLAY'. Let the pup run around to empty and to get rid of the inevitable surplus energy that all young dogs that have been kennelled always have. Once a pup has actually learned to SIT always tell it to SIT it upon arriving at the training field before giving the order 'GO PLAY'. That way you always start the training session on *your* terms and eventually you will be able to gauge what mood the dog is in for that session since, like us, their moods vary from day to day. When it has dropped a gear, call it in and put the slip lead over its head.

Hold the slip lead in the left hand and *ask* the dog to 'SIT' at the same time pushing its quarters down with the right hand. Keep that right hand hovering above its quarters ready to push them back down the instant that it tries to move. Meanwhile all the time that it is sitting fondle its ears and murmur 'Good dog SIT' and let it know that it is doing the right thing. The instant that it tries to stand up push its quarters down sharply with the sharp command 'SIT'. Back to the old black/white, good/bad. You can eventually straighten your back and stand beside the pup but be ready to correct it *immediately* it tries to 'break its drop' [get up and move unbidden.] At this early stage we are merely *asking* the dog but later on we *tell* it. With any exercise, now and forever after, it is always better to do it well for a short time or over a short distance and get it right rather than to push one's luck for slightly too long or slightly too far, thus almost inviting the pupil to get it wrong. When you consider that the pup has sat for long enough – initially for seconds rather than minutes – release it for a run round with 'Good Dog GO PLAY.' No titbits as a reward – virtue is its own reward! *Now and for the rest of that dog's life*, every time it breaks its drop, return the errant pupil to the exact position where it was sitting when it moved and explain the error of its ways or you will forever have a habitual 'creeper' which loves to play 'Grandmother's Footsteps' – or just plain 'runs in'. The other allied important point to remember is that whenever a dog is corrected for moving always ensure that the next few exercises do *not* involve movement, i.e. if a dog moves while sitting, always walk back to it on the next few occasions and 'release' it or whenever a dog runs in to a retrieve, make sure that you go out and pick that retrieve and several subsequent ones by hand in full view of the dog by way of emphasising this very basic lesson.

When, after several successive evenings, your pup is sitting confidently for a minute or more (and if you are continually correcting the pup you are pushing things too far – an easy mistake to make) drop your end of the lead and put your foot firmly on it. You then still have control unbeknown to your pupil and command it to SIT. It should by this stage SIT immediately without being pushed down. If it does, make a fuss of it and release it with lavish praise. It is essential that the trainer is completely relaxed during these (and any other) exercises. If I have an excitable pupil I go to the lake towards dusk on a summer evening with the dog on a lead. I sit down on a stump and watch the trout rising and the swallows and dragonflies skimming over the water. I become so relaxed while watching this idyllic scene that after some time of this the pupil that was wound up like a clockwork toy and sitting on the edge of its seat is also completely relaxed and is contentedly lying down. You are then starting to get there. After a few more evenings of this you can dispense with the slip lead altogether and merely accustom your pupil to sit beside you for increasingly long periods of time but be ready at all times to 'jump on' your dog and, if necessary, return it to the exact spot where it was originally sitting if it tries to move. Never be ashamed of making a fuss of your dog for a task done well whether in private or in public and never *ever* let it get away with anything. Although the SIT and HEEL are the two lessons that may be taught and reinforced *ad nauseam*, just like calling a hawk off to the fist, whenever you say to yourself with any exercise 'I'll just do it once more', *stop then* as that 'once more' is once too many and you will probably undo all your previous good work.

Once the pup is sitting instantly to the command 'SIT' it is time to introduce the whistle. Every time you command 'SIT' follow it immediately with a single, short whistle blast ('PEEP'). Eventually you can dispense with the command 'SIT' and the pup will drop to the whistle blast. Two further signals to SIT are to hold up your hand *well out to one side of your body* like a policeman holding up traffic and to stamp your foot. Both have practical applications in the field. These alternatives are again learned initially in conjunction with the command 'SIT' or the single whistle blast. So, as discussed in Chapter 5, we now have four completely different triggers for one single action which is for the dog to plant its bum firmly on the deck as soon as possible.

Remaining at the drop while you retire *(to use a quaint phrase from a nineteenth-century dissertation on 'dog breaking' or 'Sitting while you walk away' in modern parlance!)*
As soon as your pupil is sitting promptly and reliably at your feet for a reasonable length of time move on to the next lesson, sitting while you walk away, to prevent the habit of the dog running back to sit beside you every time you 'drop' it. Again, better to do this exercise well over a short distance or time span rather then to push your luck. SIT the pup, raise your hand well away from your body like the aforementioned policeman (dogs are very short-sighted and your hand will blur against your face if you do not keep it well away), look at a spot on the dog's forehead just above and between the eyes (staring directly into a dog's eyes is the precursor of a fight and should be reserved for 'rollickings') and back off just one pace. You should be able to manage this without a lead but use one if you have to. After a few seconds take one step back towards the dog, make a fuss of it and release it with 'GO PLAY'. Again, gradually increase the time and distance until you can retire out of sight. Initially you should back off facing the dog but the time will come when you can turn your back on it. However, I cheat at this stage because I keep an eye on my charge while walking away with the help of a surreptitiously held old Landrover wing mirror to prevent a game of 'Grandmother's Footsteps' developing! At first I always return to the dog and stand beside it for varying lengths of time before releasing it from the drop to prevent it from anticipating the release. This keeps it on its toes. A common mistake is to back off and *always* call up the dog to YOU. Very soon that dog is sitting with its backside hovering just above the ground in expectation of the recall because that dog knows that in two seconds, two minutes or two hours you will call it in. You are then already halfway to having an unsteady dog. Once I have established the dog awaiting my return to release it I introduce the recall whistle. I use two sets of triple short blasts ('PIP PIP PIP - PIP PIP PIP'). Thereafter I call the dog into me approximately *once* in every *four* times that we do this particular exercise but vary the order to keep it guessing. A spin-off from this is a very fast and enthusiastic return which later pays dividends with retrieving.

If you have a confirmed 'belly crawler' (and cockers are among the worst offenders at this) either 'drop' it in a retrieving alley and back off waving a thin, swishy stick just in front of its nose to keep it on the exact spot, or place a long line around its neck, pass it round a post *behind* the dog and back to you standing in front of the pupil; when you give the line a sharp jerk if the dog moves the pull is coming from *behind* the dog. As ever, any dog that 'breaks its drop' should be replaced on *exactly* the same spot that it left. You note that I do not use the command 'STAY'. This is because if I tell a dog to SIT I do not expect it to do anything else until told.

THE RECALL

A dog that will not come back when called is worse than useless. This lesson starts from puppyhood and merely involves running *away* from the pup while calling it ('HERE') or whistling to it ('PIP PIP PIP, PIP PIP PIP') and making a big fuss of it when it comes. Turning it during 'controlled exercise' and later on whistling the recall from walking away when the dog is on the drop and the turn during hunting lessons are all signals that get the dog coming back to you, followed by praise so that coming back is as enjoyable as going away from you. Again, *always* praise a dog on its return *whatever* it has been up to while away (going AWOL from the home front, chasing a hare or deer etc.) however bad tempered *you* may feel! I repeat: A dog that will not come back when called is worse than useless.

DROPPING THE DOG AT A DISTANCE

Dropping a retrieving dog and dropping a hunting dog at a distance are slightly different techniques although both types will have obviously already been taught to drop beside you. To drop a retrieving dog at some distance from you, start off, as always, with the dog reasonably close and then gradually increase the distance from you. One method is to sit the pupil and walk away. Give the recall whistle and when the dog has almost reached you suddenly blow the Stop whistle and sharply raise your arm. The pup will usually stop even if only out of sheer surprise! Initially you may have to whistle a second time or actually push its quarters down. When the dog eventually drops make a fuss of it and then whistle it in for the last few yards to emphasise the fact that it has dropped at a distance from you. If it runs right to you it is probably confused so pick it up and gently return it to the exact spot where you first whistled and blow the stop whistle gently again and back off to your original position. If it is being a bit dense about this exercise SIT it in one field and back off into the adjoining field with a stockwire fence or a gate between you. Call it in as before and, as it reaches the obstacle, blow the stop whistle and hold up your hand. The physical barrier (through which it can still see you) should inhibit it enough to stop and then drop. Again this, like a training line, is only to demonstrate what is required of the dog. When it eventually drops make a fuss of it. In time, you can open the gate between the two fields and go on from there.

When a dog is hunting or 'quartering' (of which more later) across your front, as it approaches you suddenly blow the stop whistle and leap in its path, if necessary holding up your arm in the drop position. Make the usual fuss or, as the Americans say 'Do it up big.' Once it is doing this well drop it as it approaches you and you can gradually increase the distance between you and the dog. Finally blow the stop whistle after it has just passed you, as a dog is more difficult to stop going away than coming towards you. You would be wise only to drop it once during each hunting exercise or it will soon either potter along, expecting to be dropped, or it will get bored and 'tune you out' and ignore the stop whistle altogether. However, never forget that 'A spaniel that will stop . . .'

DOWN

Pointers and setters go DOWN only, HPRs and deer dogs both SIT and go DOWN, spaniels and retrievers should only SIT but some owners like them to go DOWN as well and many dogs when told to SIT naturally prefer to lie DOWN. There is no doubt that a dog lying down is less likely to move than one that is sitting but it does make 'marking' [watching where the shot quarry fell] more difficult although many natural 'liers' will sit up to mark a bird down. A well-bred 'English' pointer or setter pup will usually go DOWN merely by the command 'DOWN' being growled at it but most other breeds have to actually be taught to do it.

Put on the slip lead and command 'DOWN'. Collapse a front leg and put your other hand on the withers pushing firmly downwards. When the dog collapses tell it 'Good dog DOWN' and all the time that it remains down continue to praise it. If it tries to get up, growl 'DOWN' and physically push it back down until it stays there. When you eventually stand up, pass the slip lead under the instep of your boot so that if you have to pull on the lead the pressure is coming from *below*. The next stage is to obtain a 'screw-in gundog tether' from your gunshop and screw it firmly into the ground. Put a long training line round the dog's neck and pass it through the tether ring which is screwed in under the dog's chin, hold the other end of the line so that there is a little bit of slack. As you back off commanding 'DOWN' you can give a sharp jerk on the line if the dog tries to either move or stand up. Once again the pressure is coming from *below* the dog's chin. The use of the training line in all these cases is only to show the dog what is required of it and once the dog has got the message the line can be dispensed with.

HEEL

There are two schools of thought about whether HEEL should be taught as one of the first lessons or as one of the last. The answer is that it depends on what job you want that dog to do. If it is destined to be a 'peg dog', a wildfowling dog, a pigeon dog or a deer dog and spend most of its working life beside the handler then I believe that HEEL should come fairly early on in its training. If, on the other hand, it is going to spend most of its time out there hunting then heelwork is better off being left until near the end. Fortunately, for some reason, walking to heel on the lead and off the lead are, to a dog, two completely separate things. Therefore if your circumstances dictate that, for reasons of safety, a dog must be on a lead between the house and the training area then teach it to walk to heel on a lead whatever its ultimate task and if it is destined to hunt then leave walking to heel *off* the lead until much later.

A right-handed Gun or Rifle's dog walks on the left whereas a falconer's dog walks on the right so that the hawk (which is invariably carried on the left fist) can see the dog easily without having to look anxiously over its shoulder. Left-handed Guns' dogs also walk on the right. A Gun's dog walks with its shoulder roughly level with the handler's leg whereas a deer dog walks to heel three-quarters of a length in front of the stalker with its hindquarters level with the stalker's leg for reasons that will be explained later. It is well worth getting this lesson 110% right, particularly with a dog that is going to spend most of its working life beside the handler, so that eventually you will just *know* that that dog is always beside you without even checking. (I was once sika stalking in Inverness-shire with a 6-year-old Labrador bitch that *never* left my side when I suddenly noticed that she was not automatically beside me. I looked back to see her on solid point on a frying pan sized patch of 'brash'. I eventually walked back and said 'What is it, Old Girl?' when she pushed her nose in and up got a woodcock! She has pointed them ever since.)

Initial HEEL lessons are best left until *after* a training session when the pupil has expended all its surplus energy. Slip the slip lead round the dog's neck like a figure '6' as usual so that the loop is self opening when slack and sit the dog tight up against a straight fence line on the left side (assuming that you are a right-handed Gun). Tie a 6 in. (15 cm) length of ½ in. (2½ cm) alkathene water pipe across the handle end of the lead with a clove hitch like a toggle. Grasp the pipe in the left hand. Command 'HEEL' and step out parallel with the fence line. As soon as the dog walks in front of or behind the required position give a *severe* jerk on the lead simultaneously commanding 'HEEL' and continue to do so until the dog is walking in the required position. The lead is *always* either slack or being severely jerked. Do not 'heave' from a taut lead situation but allow a bit of slack before the jerk. *Never* get into the 'Ben Hur' situation where you have a permanently taut lead. As the horsemen say, 'It takes two to pull.' Equally, if a dog 'hunts at heel' [walks with its nose glued to the ground] jerk the lead sharply upwards simultaneously commanding 'HEEL'. Once the dog is walking comfortably at heel you can dispense with the fence line and keep changing direction and changing your pace. It is important that the dog walks at your pace rather than *vice versa*. The next step is to lay the lead along the dog's back ready to pick it up at the slightest deviation from the correct position. Finally break off a pencil thick switch from the hedge and walk the dog at heel on the lead in the normal position. If it tries to 'pull' forward tap it across the bridge of the nose saying sharply 'HEEL'. When doing this exercise keep yourself tight up against a hedge or fence on your right hand side to prevent the dog from ducking from left to right and back again. HEEL is one exercise when I do *not* keep saying 'Good dog HEEL' because they invariably try to 'pull' forward on being praised. A lot of dogs are going to spend a lot of time walking to heel so you might as well get it absolutely correct from the word go until it becomes second nature to them. However good your dog is at walking to heel only an idiot walks it off the lead where there is traffic or unreasonable distractions.

Apart from basic retrieves and turning on the whistle this outlines the basic and all-important training for any gundog – or, for that matter, any dog. If *thoroughly* taught, the remainder of the training should be reasonably trouble free. You will probably encounter minor problems along the way but if you use your common sense and look at the perceived problem from *the dog's point of view* you will invariably work it out between you. If you have a training problem of any sort, the best way of overcoming it is frequently to leave that lesson completely alone for a week or two and when you eventually return to it it will often have sorted itself out. If, on the other hand, you and the dog have a prolonged confrontation over an exercise the dog will metaphorically dig its toes in and you will end up with a counter productive stalemate which will get neither of you anywhere. If you cannot find a way round a particular problem seek help from an experienced professional or *competent* amateur trainer. He or she will probably know of some little dodge learned from bitter experience that will do the trick.

Apart from the different HEEL position for deer dogs all of the above holds good for *any* role for which your dog is destined. However, once this is all 110% sound and you go on to the hunting, pointing and/or retrieving as the case may be, always keep in mind the eventual *main* job for your dog in terms of quarry, likely terrain, the normal capabilities of your dog's breed and begin to gradually slant its subsequent training in that direction while still sticking to the basic principles.

8: Hunting

50% of spaniels need pep pills and the other 50% need hearing aids.
The late P.R.A. (Peter) Moxon, Kennel Editor of *Shooting Times*

At the risk of stating the obvious, hunting is the method by which a dog searches a given area of ground for game in a methodical manner and then either flushes it, or points it prior to flushing it, so that it may be shot at or flown at with a hawk. However, there is rather more to it than that.

Ideally a working English springer or cocker should hunt 5-10 yd (4-8 m) either side of you and will (hopefully) eventually enter rough cover on the off chance that it might hold game. A retriever should hunt the same distance away but usually only goes into cover if it *knows* that there is game there. An HPR should hunt anything from 10 to 30 yd (9-27 m) away in woodland (again only going into thick cover if it knows there is game there) and considerably further away in the open while a pointer or setter in the open should go at least 100 yards away and preferably a lot further when searching for game. However, do not assume that any young dog knows or expects game to be present. In the early stages it is merely going through the motions of doing what it was bred to do. Eventually, as it starts to encounter live game the penny will drop but with some dogs it takes a long time for this experience to register. A great advantage of 'controlled exercise' in a gamey area with a young pup is that this will have already registered prior to serious training. The amount of live game available to you during training will have a direct bearing on how quickly this is grasped and on the dog's eventual 'game sense'. The realisation that game lives in thick cover and not on a grass field or on a ride is a major milestone in a hunting dog's life.

There is a lot of glib talk bandied about regarding 'five yards', 'twenty yards' etc. Pace it out for yourself and study it before sounding off grandly on the subject. Whoever originally perpetrated the myth that a spaniel should hunt 'within half a gunshot range' was talking utter codswallop and was responsible for a lot of potentially good spaniels being ruined! The 'official' effective range of a 12-bore shotgun is 45 yd (41 m). Pace half that distance out on the ground, look at it hard and then imagine a novice spaniel working that distance *either side* of you. Forget it! The trick of teaching any young dog to hunt is to start with the dog hunting close to you and, as you consolidate your authority over it, gradually allow it to quarter further and further away from you over a period of weeks or even months rather than days. Remember that control is like elastic – the longer it gets, the thinner it gets until it snaps! Every hunting dog has an optimum distance beyond which it is out of control. In the field this varies according to scenting conditions and the amount (and sometimes species) of game around.

When your pup is tiny, decide what its main job will be and on what sort of terrain and, particularly, how far from you it is to hunt – a dog on a well stocked pheasant shoot may well hunt only feet away whereas a pointer on a sparsely stocked moor may have to go half a mile to each side. Take three bamboo canes or whatever. Stick one in the ground to represent *you.* Stick the second as many paces to the left as you consider necessary and the third the same distance to the right so that all three are in line. Imagine a 'flat' semi-circle with the line of three canes being the base. (See Fig 1.) *Commit that distance to memory for ever.* Thereafter, whenever you take that pup out for its controlled exercise and it hits the edge of that imaginary semi-circle give a 'PIP PIP' on your whistle and walk smartly in the opposite direction. That pup will follow you and eventually will grow up believing that it never goes further from you than the radius of that semi-circle. You may walk 500 yards but over that distance the pup may well have scampered for 1,500 yards but has never been further from you than the allotted distance. At this stage it is not training but merely mental conditioning. It must learn that 'PIP PIP' means to turn towards you before you ever begin serious training.

Before you start to actually train the pup, acquire a couple of rolls of stock-fencing from a farm sale and run them out supported by stakes parallel to an existing field boundary and at the same distance from the boundary fence as the base of your imaginary semi-circle. (See Fig. 2) The length of the resulting 'corridor' should *always* face into the wind at this stage and the ground should always be 'interesting' enough (longish grass, bracken etc.) to look as though it might just hold game. As soon as the dog starts 'pottering' roll up the netting and move it elsewhere. Even the most stupid dog will soon realise that if it hunts the same old bit of ground day after day without finding anything it only goes through the motions and will soon get bored and lose enthusiasm. The object of this corridor is to bounce the dog off the sides and, because it is in an

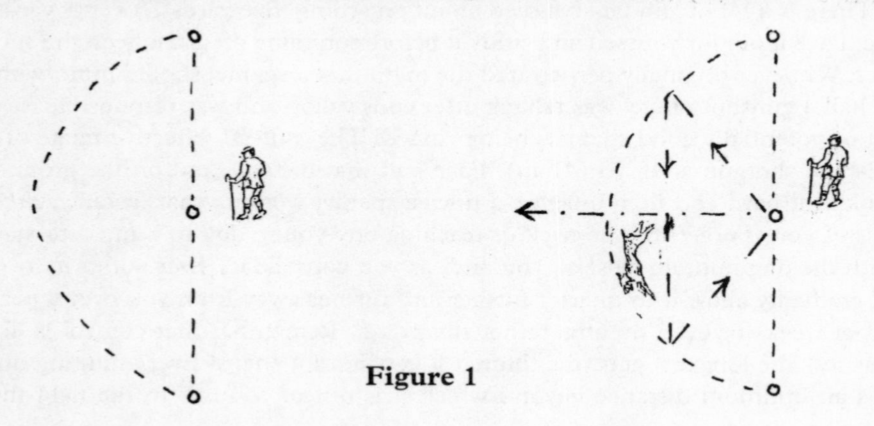

Figure 1

PLATE 7 Teaching a dog to jump an obstacle.

Teaching a Springer to respect pigeon hide construction!

PLATE 8

(below) Italian Spinone on point.

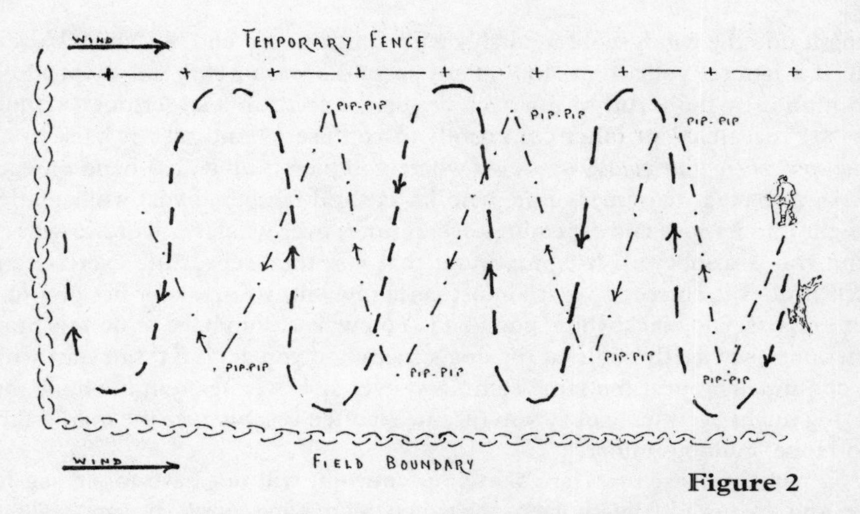

Figure 2

enclosed space, it cannot disobey you and get away with it as it could in a 50 acre (20 hectare) field. A corridor is mainly to teach a pup *how* to hunt but you are also always in control.

ACTUALLY TEACHING THE DOG TO HUNT

I allow a 'hooligan' to let off steam before teaching it to hunt, whereas with a 'wimp' I try to channel what energy it has into the lesson although, the best way to get a wimp really hunting is merely take it for a walk in a game rich area or in the rabbit pen when the penny will eventually drop, be it next week, next month or, in some cases, next year! I am never averse to letting a wimp chase the first few head of game it finds/encounters to encourage enthusiasm since it is seldom difficult to put brakes and steering on this type of dog if done at the right time. Training a dog to hunt and its subsequent hunting career is always a knife-edge balance between enthusiasm and control. In training it is like playing a fish - let it have a bit of line and then reel it in again!

Take the pupil to the centre of the corridor and sit it facing into the wind. Always 'drop' any dog before hunting it which means that you start on your terms. If you just remove the lead and the dog is away hunting immediately you have lost the initiative. Command 'GET ON' and wave your arm to the right. (Always alternate starting to the left and to the right early on.) The dog should run towards the right-hand fence. As it approaches the fence 'PIP PIP' sharply on the whistle and you go smartly towards the left-hand fence. The dog should turn and overtake you towards the left fence and as it approaches it give a sharp 'PIP PIP' and you turn smartly to the right fence again and so on. Keep its 'pattern' fairly 'flat' i.e. do not take in too much ground. All the time the dog is doing well continually praise it in a running commentary 'Good Dog. Get On. Clever Dog etc. etc.' *and as soon as* it does *not* turn on the whistle or it 'bores' straight into the wind, scold it harshly with 'AAGH AAGH' and 'PIP PIP' it back to you. If it ignores your command on any second occasion *run*, not walk, across and grab it by the scruff of the neck or slip the lead on a larger dog (without any 'SIT' or 'HERE' or other commands to confuse it) and take it back to *the exact spot where it originally disobeyed* where you pick it up with a hand on each jowl and shake it (commensurate with its age and temperament) while glaring straight into its eyes and repeating several times over whatever word or whistle command it disobeyed. It is important that you then repeat the exercise and when it does it correctly, as it almost certainly will, you make a big fuss of it thus emphasising black/white, good/bad. You will seldom have to do this more than once or twice throughout the dog's training if you get it right to start with. To continually repeat the same command over and over again in the hope that the dog might eventually obey you (as one so often sees) is ever the mark of the 'No Hope' gundog trainer.

You will be pleased to learn that you, yourself, will not have to zig-zag for ever and can gradually shorten your own quartering until you are walking straight down the middle of the corridor but remember that for every stride you walk the dog has to run 10, 20, 40 or 60 yards depending, so walk at a speed that is comfortable for the dog to operate efficiently or it will start turning downwind if you are too slow or passing behind you or taking in too much ground if you go forward too fast.

Once you have got the dog 'flowing' backwards and forwards, turning on the whistle and 'quartering' properly you can introduce the stop whistle which it has already learned during basic training. The old adage that 'a spaniel that will stop is a spaniel half trained' will soon become apparent at this stage although I personally tend to use the 'turn' whistle to keep a dog out of mischief when most trainers would use the 'stop' whistle, e.g., when a dog is 'taking in too much ground' I personally 'PIP PIP' and quarter to the *rear*. As a rule of thumb I only use the stop whistle *once* during every hunting session to prevent familiarity breeding contempt. (In my opinion most handlers over-use the STOP whistle and stifle that natural, flowing quartering that is such a joy to watch in a good hunting gundog be it a pointer or a spaniel – not to mention disrupting its concentration.) However, back to stopping it. After the dog has turned and is approaching you, blow the stop whistle sharply, stamp your foot towards the dog and shoot up your right arm simultaneously when it has almost reached you thus almost surprising/frightening the dog into dropping. If it does not sit it will certainly stop when you can firmly push it down into the SIT or DROP position and then praise it lavishly. Over the following days or weeks you can drop it further and further from you as it approaches you, then as it is passing directly across your front and eventually as it is going further and further away from you (always more difficult). Once the dog has been successfully introduced to gunfire you can do the same thing with a starting pistol, initially in conjunction with the whistle, to teach it to drop to shot.

If your dog 'bores' straight into the wind, run it backwards and forwards into the wind along a high fence which forces it to go from side to side. If your dog starts getting 'one sided', i.e., hunts out to only, say, the left without quartering on your right side at all, as soon as you see this habit creeping in move across to the left boundary and hunt it from there so it *has* to hunt to the right. Similarly some dogs will only hunt uphill of you along a bank or while others naturally hunt below you (most of Wales and Scotland is either uphill or downhill – mostly up!). Hunt along the top of the bank or along the bottom as the case may be thus forcing the dog to hunt on the less favoured side. It helps if there is a fence along the crest or valley bottom. Working a potentially disobedient dog below you on a steep bank gives you a psychological advantage because, should the dog choose to err, you can come down on it from a great height in a few strides like the proverbial ton of bricks.

When, and only when, you have the dog turning and stopping on the whistle 10 times out of 10 within the corridor can you go further afield. Choose an 'interesting' area with just a hint of game – I am lucky enough to have some shelter belts that have been brashed (the lower branches removed) and are fenced on both sides. The dog will perk up a lot once it gets into an interesting bit of gamey cover but pray that no game actually gets up at this stage (and Murphy will do his damnedest to ensure that it does!). What one is hoping for - and trying to engineer - throughout its training is a gradually increasing amount of game being presented to the dog as it learns to cope with more and more game. Game to a gundog is like oats to a horse - it revs them up tremendously and in the early stages too much game is worse than no game at all.

Good, bad or indifferent scenting conditions from day to day will also play an important part in how your dog 'goes' and at what distance from you it is under complete control. In very hot, dry weather conditions nearly all dogs will hunt listlessly and only a clown would try to hunt a pup under those conditions unless it was a real 'tearaway'. (Some 36 hours after the rain has finally come when scent improves dramatically – watch out!) Under good scenting conditions you must keep your pupil 'tighter'. As the dog's experience and therefore its all-important 'game sense' increases it will find more and more game under increasingly difficult scenting conditions as it knows where to look and how to interpret minute vestiges of scent and, if you are a shooting man, the more you eventually kill over it, the more there is to retrieve and so the more it will search for game for you to kill over it, etc., etc. I once hunted five young spaniels in early training consecutively over the same bit of woodland. The first spaniel found two rabbits, the rest none. I then took the 5-year-old family Jack Russell back over the same ground to sort out a pheasant feeder and she found another half dozen rabbits there – which she chased yipping to their buries! She had acquired game sense (too much!) but the spaniels had not. Nothing succeeds like success and this is where the partnership that you have been striving for from the outset starts to gel and you suddenly realise that you have not touched your whistle for twenty minutes and young Fido is beavering away from side to side and hunting like a good 'un. Hunting a dog under control is an ongoing thing for the rest of the dog's working life. As soon as you relax your guard it will take advantage of you and be off and, once it realises that it can do just that, you may well have lost the battle for ever. However, if you have done your initial homework soundly and *always* keep your eye on the ball this is unlikely to ever happen. If a dog is getting 'cocky' or just plain headstrong take it to a completely strange bit of ground and keep hiding. This usually knocks its confidence sufficiently for you to regain the initiative. (This is in conjunction with 'getting after it' for disobedience rather than instead of it.)

When hunting a wide ranging pointing dog in cover taller than itself - and many a hooligan spaniel that I have had through my hands would also qualify! - we can learn from our American or Continental colleagues who have far more experience with pointing dogs than ourselves and attach a special dog bell (available in any sporting goods store abroad) to the collar. I also have an ingenious American hi-tech blaze orange collar with a 'Beeper' (audible up to at least 500 yd) that 'beeps' every 10 seconds while the dog is moving but every second while the dog is on point – or stops to empty! A wide 'dayglo' collar is also invaluable for a pointer whose colour blends into the background.

A good hunting dog of any breed that is under control is an absolute joy to own whereas an out of control hooligan is a d—ned nuisance to you and to everybody else.

9: Wind and Scent

A dog with a good brain and an average nose will always find more game than one with a good nose and an average brain.
The late John ('Jack') Nash, Co. Limerick

Any dog can only know what its nose tells it. We humans live primarily by our eyes but *never forget* that a dog lives primarily by its nose. When I worked with foxhounds I always maintained that, were I granted the scenting powers of a hound for a week, I should be a lot better at my job. I have often thought the same with gundogs. We humans cannot begin to understand what goes on in a dog's nostrils. I once ran a young 'English' pointer on winter corn when it slammed on point. I roded it in for *140 yards* to a lapwing sitting on eggs! We ignore the fact that a dog's primary sense is its power of scent at our peril. I would go so far as to say that what we see as one animal, say, a rabbit is almost *four* different animals to a dog - body scent, blood scent, foot scent and carrion scent. That is why a spaniel of under one year old can hunt a bit of ground ignoring foot scent, flushing on body scent, retrieving on blood scent and then be hunted on ignoring foot scent, flushing on body scent etc. and it may come across a long dead rabbit carcase and proceed to eat it!

All this is brought about by the twin factors of wind and scent. No dog can operate efficiently, or sometimes operate at all, 'down wind' [going *with* the wind] whereas every type of gundog operates at its best 'up wind' [going *into* the wind]. Indeed a young pointing dog can only work into or, at least, across the wind, a young spaniel should only be hunted into the wind and a young retrieving dog can only find dummies into the wind because the scent of the game or dummy is being blown back to the dog's nose. It is surprising how often a supposedly experienced dog handler will try for a difficult retrieve in the field without giving the dog the all-important benefit of wind direction or does not send the dog out for a retrieve slightly down wind of the fall. A dog can pass only inches up wind of a retrieve and be *completely unaware of its existence.* Running a young pointing dog down wind will merely produce a 'long range spaniel' that will probably chase any game that it has 'bumped' into the bargain! Such are the often unpredictable vagaries of wind and scent that a pointer might 'wind' [scent] and then point a pheasant at 60 yards one day and the same dog may only wind the same pheasant in the same place at *6 in.* (15 cm.) the next. According to the Beaufort Scale wind strengths vary from Force 0 (no breeze at all) to Force 12 (hurricane) but for gundog training from Force 2 to Force 4 is about the limit. As someone who is forever stalking deer or running pointing dogs I, like any countryman, am continually aware of what the wind is doing. With practice one can soon learn to feel the wind strength and direction on one's face without resorting to wetting fingers and dropping blades of grass. A steady wind or breeze is far more valuable to a dog than gusts of varying speeds. A steady breeze, as indicated by the cloud speed and direction, is all very fine on flat, level, open ground but once one introduces the factors of hills, woods, valleys and buildings together with local variants of banks, hedges, dips and mounds things become distorted so that the wind strength and direction at human face level are often completely different from those at the dog's nose level. Wind will obviously have a bearing on what the scent does. As my friend Dick Williams of Builth Wells often says, 'Take a bonfire. Imagine the core of the bonfire is the game and the smoke is the minute scent particles. Then watch what the smoke does in relation to the wind - or lack of it.' All this means that in the early days one has to help a youngster as much as possible. This is why I run my hunting breeds of puppies 'at hack' in the middle of the local shoot (of which I am the keeper!). Only they can teach themselves about wind and scent which is where your 'controlled exercise' as a puppy comes in. Eventually, as the dog's experience grows over the years it will be able to cope with more and more adverse conditions and interpret the myriad scent messages being borne to its sensitive nose. Only then is it ready to be run down wind with confidence.

Any foxhunter will tell you that the vagaries of scent are legion and for every rule there is a large number of exceptions. As R. S. Surtees' well-known character, John Jorrocks, pronounced in *Handley Cross*, 'There's nowt so queer as scent 'cept it's a woman.' For centuries students of venery have studied this complex subject – and reached few substantial conclusions! Scent depends on humidity, ground temperature in relation to air temperature, barometric pressure, wind strength and direction and sunlight to name but a few; what may be good air scenting conditions may not necessarily be good ground scenting ones and *vice versa.* My old huntsman, the late Bob Jones, always maintained that 'If there's no scent, there's no foxes.' To put it in context, 'Any dog or hound can only know what its nose tells it.' From a practical point of view any extremes of weather will be bad scenting so do not expect any scent on very hot, cold, wet or windy days. However, most 'average' weather conditions will produce at least reasonable scenting conditions and after a few minutes the dog's body language will tell you all you need to know. Bad scenting conditions will often make a young dog potter but good conditions will rev it up. Body scent of the quarry is generally related to air scent whereas blood scent and foot scent are usually related to ground scent, but the dog still has to interpret them. So how do we convert all this theory into the practical business of actually finding game? When we hunt a dog into the wind we wish it to 'quarter' [zig zag] from side to side across our front. The further it goes to either side of us, the greater the chances of it finding game. If it 'bores' into the wind in a straight line in front of us it will only find any game on a one yard wide front whereas a dog quartering 10 yd to either side has twenty times more chance of finding game and a dog quartering 100 yd either side (see Fig. 3) has a 200/1 better chance. However the wide ranging dog may well flush the game out of gunshot range and it also has ten times more chance of being out of control! Control is like elastic . . . In thick cover in good scenting conditions where a lot of game is present then 5 yd either side is plenty, whereas in the teeth of a south-westerly gale on a 5,000 acre (2,000 ha.) heather-covered rock in Argyllshire where a covey of three was once seen within living memory then 500 yd either side is not quite enough. It is all relative but life, as they say, is one large compromise!

Obviously one cannot run a young dog into the wind *ad infinitum* and, with the very thought of running downwind being sacrosanct for a novice dog, one must resort to the stratagem of running on a cheek wind, i.e., with the wind on ones cheek or from one side (see Fig. 4). Once the trainer realises the principles of running on a cheek wind and directs the dog accordingly, even a novice dog will soon work out what is required of it especially once it has actually found some game on its beat. In fact one frequently sees a young dog competently hunting into a head wind when its pattern suddenly appears to have gone to pot. One then realises that the wind has altered and the dog has automatically compensated for it and is now hunting on a cheek wind. (This happens far more often with air-scenting pointing dogs than with ground scenting spaniels.)

When a dog is quartering it should ideally vary its pace and the 'bite' [the amount of ground it takes in at each turn] according to the scenting conditions

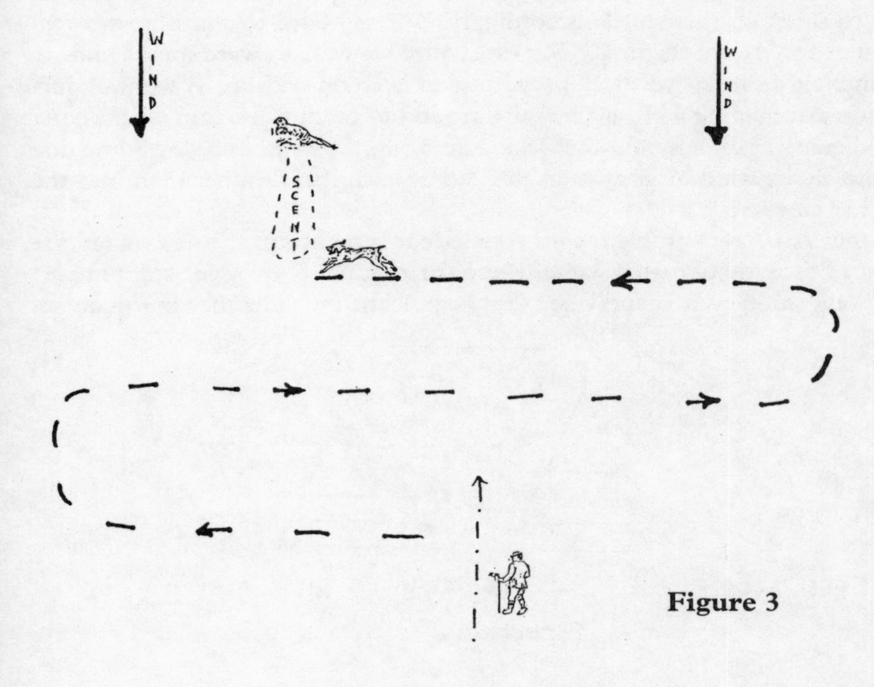

Figure 3

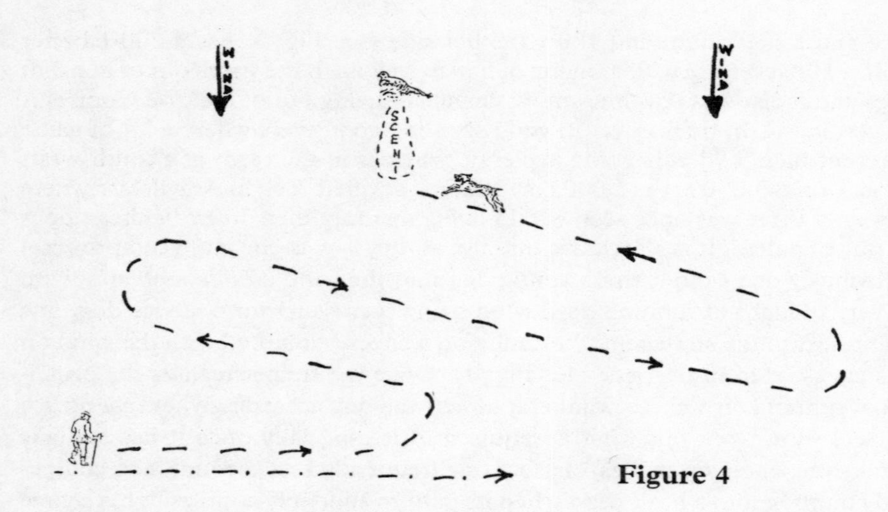

Figure 4

at the time. In bad scenting conditions it should run relatively slowly whereas in good scenting conditions it can go flat out. To put the size of the bite at its most ridiculous, if the dog can wind game at 5 yd it should take in 4½ yd and if it can wind game at 20 yd it should take in 19½ yd every time it turns – and many experienced dogs do virtually just that. However, in the early stages of training we have to do their thinking for them and, although we can do nothing about pace, we can decide roughly how much ground they should take in and turn them on the whistle accordingly. We also have to suit our own forward speed to that of the dog's. For every yard we walk forward the dog has to run anything from 20 yd to 1,000 yd just to keep up with us. If we walk forward too fast the dog will start missing ground to catch us up and we have the 'missed game triangle syndrome' *(*See Fig. 5*)* and if we go too slowly the dog will turn down wind *towards* us at the end of each 'beat' rather than into the wind, i.e. *away* from us.

Another associated problem with young dogs is pointing or 'dwelling on' the 'haunt' of recently departed game where the residual body scent still remains on the vegetation. With experience they soon learn the difference but many an

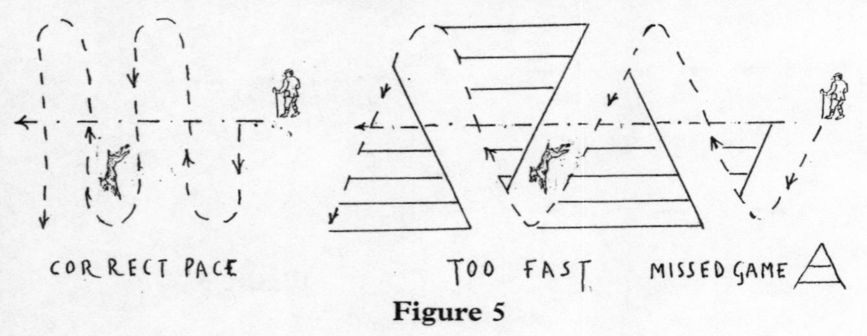

Figure 5

inexperienced trainer has been convinced that he has a 'false pointer' or a 'pottering' spaniel on his hands!

As long as the basic training is sound and the wind direction is taken into account, scent is all down to the dog's experience. In the initial stages one tries to give the pupil everything 'on a plate' but, as it gets more experienced, it learns to operate in worse and worse scenting/wind conditions until on shooting days, when scenting conditions may be everything or nothing, it frequently has to operate on virtually no scent at all! However, once again, 'Nothing succeeds like success' and the more the dog's efforts are rewarded by its interpretation of the scenting conditions being translated into actual game found (particularly if the job involves a retrieve at the end of it), the more its confidence is boosted which will result in even more game being found the next time and so on.

10: Pointing

...the chief glory of the sport is to shoot over a brace of raking pointers, matched for speed and style, sweeping over the rough places like swallows, and passing each other as if they were fine ladies not introduced.
From *The Pointer and his Predecessors* by William Arkwright, 1906

You can make most dogs hunt and you can make most dogs retrieve but you cannot *make* a dog point. Fortunately, due to the ruthless selective breeding of our forefathers ('Breed from the best and shoot the rest') we have inherited pointing breeds of gundog, both British and Continental, in which the pointing instinct is extremely highly developed. When you consider the subject matter of this book perhaps that is just as well since captive snipe, grouse and woodcock as training aids are not that easy to come by! However, given that in order to teach a dog to point one must have live game to hand, it is possible to teach the mechanics of pointing game on racing pigeons, pheasants, quail or partridges and then hope that the dogs will transfer that capability to snipe, woodcock and grouse which, fortunately, most do. Indeed, if a dog cannot or will not point a covey of grouse under decent scenting conditions, it is unlikely to point anything. Exceptions to this rule being some Irish Setters brought up solely on snipe and HPRs trained exclusively on 'fur'(for which read 'bunnies'). With any pointing dog, the greater the variety of game you can introduce it to on early on, the less chance of it being wedded to one particular species.

One can always merely run ones dog into the wind on ground that holds game and hope for the best but this system is a bit hit and miss since the dog will probably be some way away from you, will probably ' flash point' the game, will probably dive straight in and will probably chase it over the horizon to boot! On is almost certainly too far away to stage manage the proceedings, even if the dog is trailing a line, so the outcome will be a lot of unnecessary bad habits learned and no game pointed. One is better off teaching the dog to point properly but whether the eighteenth-century trainer taught 'Slut', the sow, to point partridges by the following means I know not! Last year a lady wrote to me to say how she had followed my advice in *The Versatile Gundog* and that her dog hunted, retrieved and pointed extremely well and, by the way, it was not an HPR but an Irish Water Spaniel (and I have since seen it point extremely well).

Since one needs live game in order to teach a dog to point, racing pigeons are good to start with since they have no 'game scent' therefore any mistakes are not associated with game and you do not even have to own or keep them! Your local racing pigeon fancier will hire or lend you a few pigeons or let you have some 'culls'. These can be placed in a leaf-screened wire basket or even a garden sieve, launched from a string operated or remote controlled 'pigeon launcher' or 'dizzied'. Dizzying involves the trainer putting the pigeon's head under one wing, swinging the pigeon round at arm's length two or three times clockwise followed by two or three times anti-clockwise and setting it down facing into the wind where it will remain, head under wing, until the dizzying has worn off or it is gently lifted into the air with a 5 ft hazel wand that has been acting as a position marker. The main snag with all these methods is that, whichever one is used, the pigeons will always have human hand scent on them so that, once the dog has learned to point them initially, it is unlikely to bother with anything smelling of humans thereafter.

The next step is to teach the dog to point gamebirds. If you can get hold of some, the Bob White Quail from the southern states of the USA are excellent and much better than the commercial *coturnix* quail. Between a partridge and a *coturnix* in size, the cocks have a black and white head and the hens a chestnut and brown one. When the bevy or covey is flushed in the wild they explode in a bomb burst, going in every direction to confuse predators. To counter this they have an excellent recall mechanism to bevy back up again. American gundog trainers have long harnessed this recall mechanism and one can open the cage or pen door to release a number of quail but making sure that some remain behind. The quail outside will stay reasonably close to home until flushed. The remaining quail will then start to call and those flushed will home in on the pen and go back inside *via* a 'lobster pot' one-way funnel until required for training again. They have no human hand scent on them and are 'game to order' wherever you choose to release them. They are easy to keep but difficult to obtain in the UK. I have done roughly the same thing with redleg partridges with nearly as much success but only from a static pen and not from a portable cage. Quail may be kept in the garage in a weldmesh cage on battens to let the droppings fall through. They do well on poultry layers pellets.

Much easier to acquire but needing more ground are hen pheasants (cocks will fight and are too visible). Easily obtainable as ex-layers from a gamekeeper or game farm in June/July or as poults in July/August, one wing should be hard clipped in an open topped pen with clumps of brushwood/fir brashings in it. They get pretty adept at hiding! They do well on wheat but poults will require some growers pellets to start with.

Some pointing dogs are naturally more precocious than others and many very young pups will 'sight point'. This however is a different syndrome from scent pointing. (I can never understand the thinking behind pointers abroad being taught to point by dangling some wings in front of their noses on a fishing rod and line!) I seldom *teach* dogs to point much before 8-9 months old although some are already pointing naturally by then. As with all gundog lessons one starts with the simple bit and, as the dog gains experience, one gradually 'stretches' things and makes it more and more difficult as the dog's knowledge and confidence grows. The ideal conditions for teaching a dog to point are a mild, warm, moist south-westerly breeze (about Force 2 on the Beaufort scale). Should you have to wait for weeks or even months to obtain these conditions, then so be it. It will be worth the wait.

Let the youngster run off its surplus energy before teaching it to point. Put a leather collar on the dog (preferably a wide greyhound type collar) to which is clipped a strong line about 3 to 4 yd long. Approach the game from down wind and ensure that there is nothing upwind to 'foil' the scent such as sheep or muck heaps. One is not trying to teach the dog to hunt at this stage but merely to point. As the dog encounters the scent of the game (do not forget that the wind strength and direction at the dog's level may be very different from that at your face level) you will see its ' body language' change. (Body language in a hunting or a pointing dog will tell the handler an awful lot if he has the wit to see it. In America hunters call it 'getting birdy' when a dog starts to change up a gear on acknowledging the likely presence of game in the shooting field. With practice you will learn what the scenting conditions are like, what quarry species the dog is 'winding' [scenting], how far off it is etc. etc. The great advantage that the one-dog-man has over the professional trainer is that eventually the former should be able to read his dog like a book whereas, just as the professional gets to know the dog, it goes home!) But back to basic pointing. As the dog 'hits scent', to use another American term, the trainer takes up the slack on the line. If the dog starts getting excited and jumping up and down yipping then quietly retire it from the scene and try again a few weeks later. It just it not ready for it yet. However if all goes well, as the dog gets more intent in reaching the source of this 'scent cone' the trainer gradually exerts more pressure on the line attached to the collar so that the dog is eventually restrained from any further forward movement. So we now have the situation wherein the dog is being drawn forward by this mind-blowing scent of game (The Irresistible Force) but is being firmly restrained by the trainer (The Immovable Object). This virtually compels the dog to actually go on point when the trainer can slightly slacken off the line but be ready to take up any slack immediately should the dog try to 'catwalk' forward towards the game. It is all important at this stage that once the dog goes on point it remains absolutely stationary. Later on it will learn to 'handle' game that is moving away from it and stay in contact with the game without pressurising it into flight. (My old 'English' pointer bitch will actually back off a few paces if she considers that she is pressing the covey too hard but you cannot teach them to do that.) However, in the early stages it must not move once it is on point to the extent whereby the trainer physically picks up the dog and carries it away when he considers that it has been on point for long enough. On the first two or three occasions I quietly praise the dog while it is on point but once it has got the message I keep quiet, only praising it when it has dropped to flush. There are three reasons for doing this. If you continually praise a dog when on point it may soon start pointing anything or, even worse, nothing just to be praised. If it is pointing the wrong quarry e.g. larks instead of grouse, wrens instead of pheasants etc. you are encouraging this whereas, once the quarry has been flushed, you can either praise it or gently chide it as the case may be and, thirdly, the dog is unlikely to be 'sticky' but will rode in on command to flush in anticipation of some praise. But we are getting ahead of ourselves.

Once the dog is pointing staunchly on the line is time to introduce the flush. If you continue the actual pointing for too long (how long is too long? Only the dog can tell you), the dog may well become 'sticky' and stay on point indefinitely rather than roding in on command to flush. In the first instance I keep the dog on point and flush the game with a stick, quietly but firmly dropping the dog in the DOWN position. When teaching pointing *make sure that there are no nasty associations with pointed game* in the dog's mind at any stage of the proceedings so be *tactful* if it does not drop to flush as it should. You can always go back to the drawing board on the DROP later. Only when the dog is dropping to game flushed by you can you allow the dog to flush its own game after a suitable interval on point. Click your fingers in front of the dog's nose and command 'GET 'EM UP' while controlling the speed at which the dog rodes in. A potentially sticky dog should not stay on point for too long whereas one prone to 'flash pointing' should be left for longer. If I have an unprincipled thug that tries, or is even likely to try, to ' peg' the game [grab it on the ground] I let it wear a wire greyhound racing muzzle for a few days before asking it to flush with the muzzle on. A pointer that 'mugs' its game is a confounded nuisance. A pointer that has dropped to flush is obviously already down when the shot is fired. However, when out on the training shoot I fire a .410 when ' real' game is flushed. (When grouse counting in July with older dogs I carry a .410 to salute the departing covey or some old canine stagers get a bit *blasé* about the job. But be sure not to do as I once did – I killed a grouse out of season with the .410 without thinking!)

Once you have it pointing and flushing game in an artificial situation the training game is done with so get it out into the countryside where it is likely to encounter some 'real' game but not too much. Once again, the more different species of quarry that you can get it pointing in the early stages the less likely it is to become ' wedded' to one particular species. Bird dogs should ignore 'fur' unless you particularly require them to point it. In these early outings there is no reason why it cannot still trail a line to help you to stage manage the first few points in the field but as you both gain in confidence you can eventually dispense with it. It will probably also point the ' haunt' [residual body scent of recently departed game] but that is purely lack of experience. Once it has got the message *always trust your dog's nose.* From then on, the more experience it gets in increasingly deteriorating scenting conditions the better.

11: Retrieving

The trick lies not in teaching them to retrieve, but in teaching them NOT *to retrieve.* G. W.

Go to the local park any night of the week and watch every mutt retrieve stick after stick until the owner's arm gets tired. They can all retrieve. It is only us that screw them up! We are all so obsessed that our protégé, the offspring of countless Field Trial Champions, does not let us down in the 'Shooting Field', that we usually try too hard for the pup's own good. When once researching an article for the Retriever Championship it soon became apparent that the previous five winners had all used that hi-tech, state of the art aid, the tennis ball, sparingly but intelligently in every sort of acceptable cover to make it both interesting and fun for the young puppy. At that stage they were 'asking' them. Only later, when the youngster was retrieving well, did they 'tell' them.

Most gundogs of whatever breed will retrieve. Even our 'English' pointer pups are forever raiding my wife's tack room for sponges and dandy brushes! A current GWP pup is a natural marker with a wonderful mouth while my seventh generation Labrador pup is so far completely disinterested! However, she will be picking up next season. Abroad, many gundogs are 'force retrieved' – a method involving pain until they retrieve – and indeed in America even natural retrievers are 'force retrieved'. I find that the two tricks with 'iffy' retrievers are, firstly, to find something that they *enjoy* carrying even if one has to resort to a meaty bone if all else fails (although most find my hawking glove sufficiently revolting to be attractive), and secondly, once it is actually retrieving, to do it little and not very often. The problems arise from the two main handler faults of giving pups far too many boring retrieves and from steadying them up [preventing them from retrieving until commanded] too early on. The only retrieve that a pup should be able to actually see in the open is its very first one and thereafter they should all be in light cover (long grass, bracken, etc.) and into the wind. Paradoxically, the more a dog has to work for its retrieve (within reason), the better job it will invariably make of it. The same with water retrieves. One session on the millpond and then on to the river/stream. While on the subject of boring retrieves, the ubiquitous bog-standard canvas dummy is about the most boring object of the lot. The 'retrieverholic' will retrieve anything anyway but to an 'iffy' retriever they must be like dry bread and water. Use your imagination: 'barrel skinned' rabbit skins air dried and shrunk onto small logs of wood, dried pigeon, duck or pheasant wings fixed to a firm base with elastic bands, rolled-up bits of carpet, tennis balls, car radiator hoses and old dandy brushes kept in one's game bag with dead rabbits and pigeons, these are the tools of the retriever trainer. The more attractive to the dog the dummy is, the less likely they are to spit it out, although rabbit skin dummies become very slimy when wet. By all means have the odd canvas dummy for water work – they float better than a sand filled 'squeezee' bottle!

I give all my pups their initial retrieves in a narrow 'alley' between two lines of stock wire with a dead end. That way they *have* to bring the dummy back to me and thereafter it never occurs to them to do otherwise. Across the end of the 'alley' I dig several parallel trenches 4-5 in. (10-12 cm) deep forming a series of small ridges and valleys into which the dummy falls out of sight of the pupil. I throw the dummy along the alley with the command 'HI LOST' thus associating that particular command with something to be retrieved (*and nothing else*) right from the outset. I then keep quiet (apart from murmuring the occasional 'Good Dog' as required), crouch down on its return with my gaze centred on the middle of its 'forehead' and gradually back away as it approaches me. By keeping quiet I do not interrupt its concentration, by crouching down I encourage rather than intimidate it (and I am less likely to 'clock' it round the ear with my bag of dummies!), by averting my stare I do not challenge it for possession and by backing away I forestall it dropping the retrieve before it is in my hands. Taking the dummy gently but firmly with both hands (avoiding painfully tweaking its whiskers) I quietly command 'DEAD' and very gently roll the dummy towards me. In most cases the pup will release it. Should the occasional pupil hold on to it, I blow sharply down its nostrils (like blowing out a candle) and it will let go. Either way I then make a big fuss of it. I use a number of different dummies from the outset to prevent it from becoming wedded to a particular type.

When the pupil is sufficiently keen on retrieving anything thrown for it, I sit it in the alley, back off some ten paces and throw the dummy over my shoulder to land down the alley. (This takes a bit of practice!) If the pup tries to run in for the dummy I am in a position to intercept the errant hound and firmly sit it back on the exact spot where it was first dropped with the command 'HUP' repeated. I then throw several more dummies down the alley which I pick up by hand, throwing them up in the air and catching them so the pupil is fully aware that I have retrieved them myself. Once the pupil is sitting steadily to the thrown dummy, I throw four and pick up three dummies myself for each one I ask the dog to retrieve. I use a considerable array of dummies. The person with only one dummy will always have an unsteady dog because that dog soon knows that in two seconds, two minutes or two hours it will be sent for 'the dummy' and is poised to retrieve it. Once the lesson that the pupil *only* retrieves on command is learned 110% one can dispense with the alley and repeat the exercise in an open space.

Having mastered the basics, the rest of the retrieving lessons begin to be slanted towards the particular branch of shooting for which that dog is ultimately destined and, sooner or later, this involves 'cold game'. Cold game is dead game that has been shot previously by the trainer or purchased from the game dealer and in either case kept in the freezer until required. You will need several items of cold game since, although you can use the same item for several dogs, you cannot keep on using the same item for one dog. They will soon give up. Dead grey squirrels with the claws nipped off are excellent first retrieves and I find that incompletely thawed out rabbits still have enough firmness to give the dog confidence but get it on to your eventual quarry as soon as possible. Prior to freezing, game should be in pristine condition, i.e., cleanly shot with no blood on it, frozen before it becomes high and not messed about so that the fur or feathers lie close to the body and look like they do on the live quarry. Thaw out the cold game, beg or borrow a pair of nylon tights and cut them into convenient lengths. Push the cold game into the length of tights and tie a knot at each end. Sit the dog and throw an ordinary dummy as usual. When the dog has successfully retrieved it, sit the pupil again, rub your hand scent over the cold game clad in tights and throw it as per the dummy. Send the dog after a short interval and keep quiet (except for murmuring the occasional encouragement as appropriate). You will get one of a number of reactions. You may be lucky and have a straight retrieve to hand *or* it may mouth it, pick it up and drop it; retrieve it half way back and drop it; sniff it and come straight back without it or just plain eat it! Do not be (too) despondent . . . it happens! Taking it to a pond and throwing it as for basic waterwork often works and intercept the subsequent retrieve at the waterside. Failing a pond, walk the dog at heel, let it see you throw the cold game to one side in light cover as you walk past; when you have continued for about twenty yards with the dog still at heel, send the dog back with 'HI LOST' *and keep walking on*. Or standing in the gateway of a stockwire fence and sending the novice down one side of the fence for the cold game, with an experienced dog a few seconds later down the other side, brings the jealousy/competition element into it. (The fence should prevent the novice being 'mugged'.) In each case give the recall whistle *as soon as* the dog's head goes down to the cold game and walk briskly away. By a combination of different cold game species and different techniques you will eventually win and then you are away. However, d*o not* keep lobbing the same old 'manky' pheasant (or whatever) in the same old place without it being retrieved or you will sicken the dog to death. Once the dog has retrieved its first cold game make a big fuss of it and possibly try it once more elsewhere with something different *and leave it at that.*

In *The Versatile Gundog,* and umpteen Labrador books, are described many 'fancy retrieving tricks' but the only one you need worry about here for practical purposes is 'Getting Back'. This teaches the dog to keep going out in a straight line for ever or until told to stop just down wind of the retrieve and can obviously be taught with dummies. Sit the dog at heel beside a fence line or, better still, in a 'green lane' (droving lane). Walk it forward down wind at heel along the fence or lane and after a few yards let it see you toss a dummy into

Taking a dead mallard from a wildfowling pupil.

PLATE 9

A good conversion from stable to kennel.

Picking up grouse.

PLATE 10

A selection of deer dogs in training (the Brittany was RTU'd).

light cover just to one side. Keep walking on along the fence with the dog at heel and after 20 yd drop the dog and walk on alone for five more paces. Turn to face the dog and command 'HI LOST. GET BACK' and direct it with your arm (eventually the dog will learn gun sense and take the direction from the gun barrel) back along the fence/lane towards the dummy into the wind. It should eventually remember that the dummy had been dropped earlier and go back for it (or it may just stare uncomprehendingly at your outstretched arm!). As it runs back towards the dummy keep commanding 'GET BACK' until it reaches the dummy and retrieves it to you. Go back and repeat the exercise three or four times on a 'marked' [seen] retrieve in exactly the same spot but extending the distance gradually each time. Over several days you can repeat this exercise without overdoing it but each time gradually extending the distance. It is vitally important that it succeeds in finding the dummy, aided by the wind direction, every time. From there it is a short step to hiding the dummy on the exact spot where all the previous marked dummies were dropped and sending the dog back on an unseen retrieve from about 20 yd and thereafter again gradually increasing the distance. You can eventually dispense with the fenceline or lane and send it back in the open towards a point some yards downwind of the retrieve and, as it hits the scent, should turn into the wind for the dummy/game. The dog will experience at least one hiccup along the line when you will have to go (metaphorically) backwards to consolidate the last step but, once mastered, this method saves a lot of legwork later on.

Once you have got the basic retrieving and cold game soundly under both your belts, the quicker you get on to your chosen quarry the better (game seasons permitting), since practical experience in the field is the greatest tutor of them all.

12: Dogs for Grouse

12 August - 10 December*

The better the dogs, the better the day.
Grouse Shooting in *Elements of Shooting* by Eric Parker, 1924

The red grouse *(lagopus scoticus)* occurs on heather moorland from Dartmoor (where it was introduced in the nineteenth century and still maintains a tenuous foothold) to the Shetlands. If the popular press is to be believed grouse are only shot on the Glorious Twelfth and deep in the Highlands at that and, indeed, many shooting men are only concerned with them up until mid-September but of course the season runs up until nearly Christmas. Grouse are found in extremely varying densities in England, Ireland, Wales, Scotland and the Isle of Man and heather forms 90% of their diet. Grouse pair up in the winter and establish their breeding territories until the following autumn with the hen laying in late March/early April depending on latitude and altitude. Should she lose a clutch of eggs she will lay another clutch which accounts for youngsters from 'cheeper' size up to almost adult size in August. A 'barren pair' is, of course, a pair that lays a clutch but loses either eggs or chicks due to weather or predators. As the young grouse in the covey get older the territories become less important. The naive coveys of August are a far cry from the streetwise battle hardened veterans of October and November which are infamous for ducking and diving, running and hiding to avoid being flushed. Paradoxically, in relatively still weather they will allow one to almost tread on them before flushing whereas in wild, windy weather, when the cock grouse has his head almost permanently above the heather on the lookout for predators, they will be up and gone several hundred yards in front of one. Many a time has my game book recorded a windy day with the dreaded HOSFOD (Head Over Skyline, Fly/Flip [or whatever] Off Downwind'!). Obviously a slight breeze is ideal for walking them up whereas they can still be driven, and frequently drive well, on windy days.

Traditionally, shooting an old blackcock 'in the blue' was like cutting a good stick from the hedge – one took one's chance when offered! However, one should remember that the blackgame season opens for historical reasons on 20 August. A greyhen and her brood 'hold' tighter than grouse and in flight they superficially resemble a covey of grouse but the distinctive wingbeat is slower and the chicks flush in ones and twos. Should one commit the ultimate *faux pas* during the first week of the grouse season the featherless legs and feet of the

*All game dates given are for England, Wales & Scotland. Northern Ireland differs.

blackgame will confirm the gamekeeper's gleeful claim to a fine! However, a brood of blackgame found on the 'hill edge' or on a recently afforested moor is a great nursery for a young pointing dog.

Grouse shooting falls into three separate forms: driven grouse shooting, 'walked up over dogs' which was once synonymous with being walked up over pointers and setters but is now usually taken to mean over spaniels and retrievers and, by way of differentiation, 'walked up over pointers' which is a general term for shooting over any pointing breeds, be it 'bird dogs' plus retrievers or HPRs. There are also bastard combinations of these like walking up over spaniels with pointers ranging out to the flanks, stand-and-drive grouse shooting and others. Neither must one forget game hawking over pointers with falcons. Furthermore there are usually two different types of heather moorland. Driving moors invariably employ full-time keepers who burn patches of heather annually in rotation to produce a patchwork of different aged plants to ensure food, cover for nesting and shelter from predators. These manicured moors are a lot easier on dogs since they have relative 'putting greens' at regular intervals upon which to work. Where the heather is interspersed with 'white grass' the going is even easier. On the other hand most walked up moors have experienced little or no burning and are a continuous sea of knee high mature heather with stems as thick as your finger that seek to trip one at every stride. These are extremely hard going for both man and dog and have humbled many a sportsman who prided himself on being fit!

What of the dogs? I am not talking here so much of the gundog belonging to someone who enjoys his or her annual day or week 'on the grouse', when they will probably take their dog anyway, but of dogs belonging to the person for whom grouse work is a major factor in their sporting calendar. Grouse appear to have a strong and attractive scent for dogs and the nearly all dogs really seem to enjoy grouse work. Fitness is a *sine qua non* and not always easily achieved after a long relaxing summer. A good nose is of paramount importance, particularly in August since most dogs' noses will be filled with pollen from the heather. The ability to work in the hot sun will favour the shorter coated breeds and one should always be aware that the threat of heat exhaustion is never far away. Colour on 'the hill' is a secondary consideration but a liver-and-white flecked GSP or wirehair on point often takes some spotting. A white dog is very visible but 'jumpy' grouse will not hold as well to a light-coloured dog as a dark one. Size, however, is important and in this context I shall repeat that 'a good big 'un will always beat a good little 'un'. 'Short legs and long heather very seldom go together' as the old rhyme has it.

DRIVEN GROUSE

On a driven day there are two completely different jobs for the dogs. There are the beating dogs and there are the picking up dogs, some of which will be owned by the Guns themselves and others by the pickers up. First the beating dogs. These must be extremely fit and with tremendous stamina since they are on the go in the glaring sun several days a week for most of the day and each drive is often well over a mile long. I am a great fan of spaniels and have known some spaniels that were great on grouse but if you look at 'the line' during a drive it is invariably the spaniels that have fallen in at heel first. They are basically too small however large their heart, bless them, their bustling action saps their energy quickly and in the heat they are carrying too much coat. (Many people now clip their spaniels right out in the early summer particularly the ears. It looks a bit odd but it keeps them free from skin parasites and they can stand the heat better.) However, where a lot of heather burning has been carried out spaniels can usually manage with the rest. A grouse beating dog must range a lot wider than its woodland counterpart which sometimes causes a snag for young dogs when they go on the pheasants later on. As has been seen in the hunting chapter (Chapter 8), the trick is to start them hunting close in and then gradually let them work further away from you as you consolidate your authority over them. Grouse work therefore goes directly against this basic training principle. My personal preference for grouse beating dogs would be for large, powerful, short-coated dogs such as Labradors, GSPs or Weimaraners. The latter two breeds can be taught to work downwind purely as flushing dogs rather than as pointing dogs, although if worked into the wind they should be able to point as well and they naturally cover a lot more ground than a hunting lab. Grouse beating is a great school for a young dog since everything takes place in the open and everyone is at a distance, the dog is in continual view of the handler (and knows it!) and most keepers are understanding enough if one has to run forward of the line to remonstrate with a wrongdoer. 'Dropping to flush' is one of the most important lessons to *thoroughly* teach a beating dog since flushed grouse fly temptingly low and, if chased by a dog which inadvertently then flushes the next covey and so on, the grouse will cross the butts as one large pack thus giving the Guns only one opportunity for a shot.

Picking up dogs are subjected to less physical hard work than beating dogs since they are static for most or all of the drive although theirs is no sinecure either. Any dog from a breed that retrieves will, with experience, become a competent retriever of grouse although, as ever, some will invariably turn out better than others. Most dogs enjoy the challenge of picking up grouse and a lightly wing tipped bird in thick, high heather is a stern test for any retrieving dog. The ability to mark accurately and to use their noses comes high on the list of requirements particularly when there is little breeze and their noses are full of pollen. Many experienced grouse dogs have the ability to *know* when a bird in the covey has been hit and flies on with the rest to suddenly fall half a mile or more behind the butts. (I personally believe that they *hear* the pellets strike the feathers.) Mike Prosser's GSP x springer, Sam, was well known in Yorkshire for sitting by himself several hundred yards back to deal with just such a bird. (Unfortunately pheasants frequently do exactly the same thing but the trees prevent one from seeing them come down.) Accurate marking on the hill by the handler too is equally essential and one hopes that there is a prominent reference point (which there seldom is!) to help one. A stone dead grouse that falls into a clump of heather without bouncing appears to give off virtually no scent for the first 30-45 minutes and takes some finding. Stick your thumbstick in at the exact spot where you think the bird is down and, if possible, get a 'cross mark' from another picker up to verify it and then hunt a young dog back into the wind towards the fall. As with all retrieving for the tyro, nothing succeeds like success. 'Hoovering up' behind, and then in front of, the butts after a busy drive is sometimes the only way to account for all the grouse down and, with experience, retrieving dogs soon learn to 'sweep' the area into the wind spread out as a pack. When a Gun is fortunate enough to be in the hot seat he may be forgiven if his memory is not as accurate as his picker up may have wished. When 'hoovering', the handler should be ready to step in quickly should a young dog try to mug another dog's retrieve. Where the heather has been regularly burned behind the butts to facilitate picking up, the pickers up should respect the Guns' wishes to work their own dogs and leave that area for them. With more and more driven days being sold by the brace (and £100 a brace at that) good grouse dogs are in demand and incapable (as opposed to inexperienced) ones are not invited twice. (Idle or coffee-housing pickers-up seldom get asked a second time either!)

WALKING UP OVER DOGS

This is an extremely pleasant and relaxed, if tiring, way of shooting grouse. I have been known to remark after slogging up – one never seems to go *downhill* at this job – some of those Perthshire hills under a glaring sun all day in pursuit of seemingly non-existent grouse, that grouse shooting is rather like knocking one's head against a wall - it is great fun when it stops! Walking up grouse over dogs is not expensive, it is great fun and it puts grouse shooting within reach of most people's pockets. However, I cannot over-emphasise to anyone who has not yet had the good fortune or, indeed, the privilege of walking up grouse just how quickly a covey is 'up and away'. Unless Guns are eternally vigilant and ready to take their opportunities as soon as they present themselves they will start to wonder why they ever bothered to carry a gamebag!

Walking up is normally done by parties of 6–10 British or foreign Guns having their annual trip to 'the hill' together with keepers, husbands, wives, girlfriends, lovers, sons, daughters, Uncle Tom Cobley and all together with their dogs. It all makes for a very enjoyable day's sport. One can scale it down and one or two Guns and a spaniel can still have a lot of fun but the sheer mathematics of two-men-and-their-dog on 10,000 acres looking for 'the covey' stacks the odds against success. Reasonably priced shooting is not difficult to come by after the premium first week of the season and provides a lot of people with an awful lot of fun as well as widening the sporting horizons of many Guns and their dogs brought up on 'bread and butter' pheasants. If the Guns are from abroad they probably all shoot over dogs themselves at home and they very much miss having their own dogs with them although, under the new quarantine regulations, this is now possible. They also possibly know quite a bit about dog work so the keeper should be aware that he is very much an ambassador for the standard of gundog work in Britain. Indeed, some foreign Guns seldom used to miss an opportunity to remind us of how superior their dogs at home were to our ineffectual, lumbering brutes but now that are allowed to bring over their own dogs they are a little quieter on the subject! In fact the foreign falconers in Caithness this summer ended up using our dogs and leaving their own in kennels!

If one is going to enjoy one's day and not be embarrassed by letting the side down, each Gun should be reasonably fit. Unfortunately all the jogging and gym work in the world are a waste of effort and the only way to get fit for walking on the hill is to walk on the hill. The only possible alternative is to walk or, better, run up the stairs of an office/tower block two steps at a time every day for a few weeks beforehand (keep details of the nearest cardiac arrest unit handy!). The old adage of 'He who walks the furthest shoots the most grouse' is very apposite. Again fitness also applies to the dogs. For the sake of safety the keeper must ensure that 'the line' is militarily straight at all times, particularly when people are getting tired, even if the pace is that of the slowest man. We have all experienced some hairy moments when the line has straggled and a covey has got up behind the guns. The shooting party should be quiet and the dogs hunting well within range because when a covey explodes out of the heather one has very little time in which to get ones shot off before they are out of range. One's shotgun should only be held in either of the two classic walking positions if one is going to have any chance of a shot at all and after the dogs have put in so much effort to actually produce a covey it is only right that they should be rewarded with a retrieve. When one gets into the 'thumb up bum and mind in neutral' stage and is carrying one's fowling piece by the barrels over one shoulder or at the 'short trail' is precisely when a large covey erupts at one's feet and goes cackling away unsaluted over the distant horizon giving the grouse equivalent of 'two fingers'!

The dogs in the line are usually something of a hotch potch but inevitably spaniels and Labradors form the bulk of them. I have also seen terriers, dachshunds, Great Danes, English mastiffs, Dalmations and Rhodesian ridgebacks out to mention but a few. But with foreign Guns it is invariably only ones own gundogs doing the work. I once took out a party of eight enthusiastic European Guns. The *modus operandi* was to work a couple of spaniels in front of the line with a brace of pointers working out on the flanks beyond the line of Guns. Frowned on by the purists but effective nevertheless. A pointer eventually slammed on point, I dropped the other dogs and went forward to the point with two nominated Guns as per my briefing in my 'fluent' rendering of their native language. I was concentrating on the usual three dimensional situation – the young dog holding its point, the other dogs remaining down, the grouse 'jumpy', the two Guns in the correct position *vis-à-vis* the pointer, etc., etc. When all was ready I roded in the pointer and up got the covey. I and the dog were instantly deafened by the fusilade of 16 almost simultaneous shots. There was no way that the other six Guns were going to be denied their first opportunity of shooting *'les groos'*! There has to be a moral there somewhere and I am glad that I did not have to eat the result of their combined marksmanship!

It is not really important which breeds of dog are used for walking up as long as they are sufficiently well trained to hunt no more than ten yards in front of the line. Much further and the grouse are out of range before anyone has fired a shot. To have a dog that is frankly out of control is extremely selfish towards ones fellow Guns and I blanch at the sight of a Gun being towed round the moor by a canine hooligan attached to his belt. That *is* a recipe for disaster. Another major fault is to have a dog that is not 'steady to flush'. Because grouse usually fly away low, hugging the ground to avoid aerial predators, a dog in hot pursuit of the covey will either inhibit a neighbouring gun from taking a shot at all or ensure that one's dog gets a charge of shot in the back of the head. Either situation can seriously damage relationships! Walking up over dogs is great fun and takes one to some of the most wonderful scenery in Britain. It is also a great school for young dogs having their first taste of the real thing.

WALKING UP GROUSE OVER POINTERS

This form of shooting is, to me, among the cream of gameshooting and bettered only by flying peregrines at grouse over pointers. However, it is a somewhat selfish sport since only two Guns actually shoot over the point while the dogs are usually worked by a separate (unarmed) handler. In fact on some estates it is the norm for Guns to walk unloaded until a dog actually comes on point, when the handler then instructs them to load as they approach 'the moment of truth'. This custom I often feel is brought about by self-preservation following the excessive enthusiasm of foreign Nimrods! Dog work rather than marksmanship is what it is all about because when somebody says, 'on the word *go* a covey of grouse will get up in front of you and fly directly away' one could be tempted to think the shooting is on par with DTL clays. I would that it were that straightforward!

Shooting over 'English' pointers or setters was traditionally the way grouse were shot in August with the pointers going south to the partridge manors of England in September. Nowadays some moors with a reasonable stock of birds walk them up in August and then drive them once they have become 'streetwise' and will no longer lie to the point. Some driving moors that have cancelled driven shooting in a bad grouse breeding year will let a few days over pointers to recoup some of the horrendous costs involved in running a moor. Indeed, owning a Scottish estate has been likened to standing under a cold shower while tearing up £20 notes! But walking up grouse over pointers traditionally occurs when there are insufficient grouse to warrant driving them, too spread out for walking them up over dogs or the ground is unsuitable for driving them. A team of ten assorted Guns and non-combatants walking 15 yd apart still only covers (you've guessed!) 135 yd whereas a 'good going' pointer will cover that distance and more on *either side* of the handler. Since the art (and it most certainly is an art) of driving grouse relies on their propensity for following natural contours in flight the flat moors of Caithness and Sutherland, which are more reminiscent of the west of Ireland than the Highlands have long been considered the Mecca for pointer work.

In Britain our pointers and setters are not required to retrieve shot game although they do so in every other part of the world. I, personally, do not let my own pointers retrieve for their first two seasons, when I use a Labrador but after that I allow them to retrieve any grouse that they have pointed and produced on command. Retrieving seems to come naturally to my line of 'English' pointers but I cannot speak for anyone else's. Most setters are more natural retrievers than 'English' pointers. I am never ashamed to let my first season pointers trail a 4-5 yd line on shooting days since the aforementioned advantages far outweigh any possible disadvantages. Although I keep talking about 'English' pointers and setters, many Guns now shoot over the continental HPRs which should also retrieve their game and therefore one can dispense with the services of a retriever. Although HPRs cover considerably more ground than a spaniel does, very few cover the amount of ground that a pointer or setter will. However, once the grouse season is over most HPRs will be busy on pheasants, partridges and ground game while quite possibly also assisting with the doe cull as well, none of which the traditional 'bird dogs' are likely to be involved with.

Pointers and setters tend, in practice, to have a relatively short season on their traditional quarry compared with other gundogs whereas there are great opportunities for working them on snipe and, later on, woodcock at which they soon become extremely adept. The fact that a covey of grouse must give off a mind blowing scent compared with that of a small wader does not seem to stop them winding snipe and woodcock at equally considerable distances. I must stress that walking up grouse over pointers is all about dog work rather then marksmanship. The sight of a matched brace of pointers of any breed flowing effortlessly backwards and forwards over the heather unravelling the most minute vestiges of scent until one dog slams on point as though cast in stone and is impeccably backed by its bracemate should send shivers up the spine of any true dogman. The subsequent shot or shots is almost coincidental to the enjoyment of witnessing classic dog work at its best.

It is not for nothing that the red grouse has long been known as 'The King of Gamebirds'.

13: Dogs for Snipe

12 AUGUST – 31 JANUARY

Maria [Major Yeats' Irish Water Spaniel] became possessed of seven devils and broke away from heel the first time I let off my gun, ranging far and wide in search of the snipe I had missed, and putting up every live thing for half a mile round, as she went splashing and steeplechasing through the bog.
The Irish RM and His Experiences, Somerville and Ross, 1928.

The common snipe *(gallinago gallinago)* has the longest season of any gamebird (for, although waders, snipe are legally 'game') and can add spice to many a grouse day and liven up a duck flight. The diminutive and far less common jacksnipe and the larger and extremely rare great snipe are now protected by law but the common snipe abounds on the foreshore, in boggy ground on either low ground or moorland, sewage outlets and anywhere where its long bill can probe in the soft ground for invertebrates (worms and creepy crawlies to thee and me!). Water meadows on which cattle have summered are a favourite haunt of theirs, since cow dung encourages the presence of worms and bovine hoofprints form the 'mini bogs' that are ideal for snipe. We have a tennis court sized boggy field here which, for reasons best known to themselves, is often good for 30-40 snipe around Christmas time. Once blood from the local slaughterhouse was spread on bogs to encourage worms and therefore snipe! Unfortunately, a lot of former wetland in Britain has now been drained in the interests of agriculture or turned over to commercial garden peat production and no longer holds a single snipe. Although the UK has a resident breeding population (the evocative drumming of displaying snipe has to be heard to be believed), the main winter population here flies in from their insect-rich breeding grounds of Scandinavia and beyond the Arctic Circle on the full September and October moons – a full month or more before their larger cousins, the woodcock. Snipe initially make their landfall on our north eastern coastlines which is bereft of them one day and the next morning they are thick as fleas on a dog! However, as winter and hard weather progress, they work their way south and west to those islands and peninsulas of the British Isles that are warmed by the Gulf Stream where they can still probe for worms.

These diminutive, dart shaped feathered missiles always appear to a Gun to have a lot of air around them as they explode singularly, in pairs or even in a *wisp* with their characteristic *zig-zag* flight and a loud *scaarp scaarp* and disappear into the wide blue yonder towards a distant horizon! (The jack snipe, however, will usually fly for a mere 50 yards before landing again.) Kills to cartridge ratio can prove embarrassing to even the most experienced of Guns! Like grouse, snipe are 'up, up and away' before an unprepared Gun can get his 'smokepole' to his shoulder so they need to 'rise' well within half a gunshot range. Albeit extremely small in size – it takes a lot to make a decent meal even with the *trails* left in – they appear to give off a disproportionately strong scent and, once the dogs work out that they are legitimate quarry, most pointing dogs will point them. Although many dogs initially find them unattractive to retrieve, most eventually come to love working with them. The trick with a dog averse to retrieving them is to pick a dead snipe by hand, rub one's hand scent all over it and then throw it like a dummy. Most dogs then soon get the message. However, a snipe that has fallen stone dead into a tiny hollow, with the breeze blowing straight over the top of it, will take some finding by even the most experienced snipe retriever. Because they are so small one frequently thinks that the dog has come back without one, particularly in the gloaming, until one notices a tiny leg or bill protruding from the dog's mouth! Like grouse they will sit tight one day and get up 50 yards in front the next and although they were frequently driven over the Guns up until the nineteen fifties, they are usually walked up on most snipe grounds nowadays with several notable exceptions. However, the long debated discussion on the merits or otherwise of driving snipe up or down wind will continue to be discussed until Doomsday itself!

What of the dogs? As any Irish snipe shooter will tell you, 'until both boots are full, you cannot concentrate on the job in hand.' So with the dogs. Some dogs positively hate getting their feet wet, some will put up with it and others just love it. A snipe shooter's dog should absolutely revel in being up to its elbows in thick, glutinous, smelly mud and the muddier, the merrier! Most breeds are suitable for snipe shooting if used within their *modus operandi*. 'If they're good enough, they're big enough' and colour is immaterial. Overall, snipe are more likely to get up ahead of the dog than to sit tight when they are often 'walked over'. Remember that if a point appears to be unproductive the snipe is as likely to have circled *back* behind the dog and/or Gun as to have moved forward. With inexperienced (and often perplexed) dogs I whisper quietly 'CAST BACK' and gently 'nudge' the dog in a rearward circle when they will often fresh-find their quarry. With experience they eventually work it out for themselves. Either a close working flushing dog, be it a spaniel or a retriever, or a pointing dog with a 'long nose' is the ideal snipe dog. With spaniels or retrievers I must emphasise *close working* if any success is to be anticipated and, if its nose is not exceptional, a fairly pedestrian pointer will also do the job. Any of the setters will do well but when one talks of dogs for snipe, the words 'Irish Setter' are whispered almost with reverence! As I have already said, as the rabbit is to the spaniel, so is the snipe to the Irish Setter – The Good Lord almost created the one to complement the other – and 'the red dogs' will conjure up snipe after snipe where any other breed would convince you that none existed! However, the flip side is that it is often found that many Irish Setters, if initially trained exclusively on snipe, will ignore virtually all other game thereafter. Most setters can be encouraged to retrieve them whereas a number of dogs of all breeds seem to have a predilection for swallowing whole the first few they encounter!

Like wildfowling dogs, arthritis is the great enemy. No amount of the customary towelling will really get a dog dry although the towelling zip-up 'sleeping bags' appear to be very effective. A 4 x 4 ft (1.2 x 1.2 m) wooden apple or potato 'bin' or smaller equivalent with a weldmesh lid filled with wheat (definitely *not* barley) straw in the garage into which the dog can be put for a couple of hours on ones return home before putting it to bed will get it really clean and dry. (Burying titbits in the straw really gets them burrowing!) The bin can be stored on its side to save space. The straw must be burnt on the bonfire once it gets past it. Although I firmly believe that one does a young snipe or wildfowling dog no favours by keeping it permanently in a warm house beside the fire and then expecting it to put up with wet, icy shooting conditions, all our senior shooting dogs eventually graduate to living beside the Aga! There are very few dogs kept purely for snipe work outside Ireland but this occasional, yet nonetheless pleasant, sideline is yet another shot in a working gundog's locker. Snipe are delicious to eat but, as the old cookery books say, 'First shoot your snipe'!

14: Dogs for Wildfowling

1 SEPTEMBER - 31 JANUARY
(OR BELOW THE HIGH WATER MARK UP UNTIL 20 FEBRUARY)

There are times when the bond between man and dog is particularly intense but none more so than when sharing the solitude of the wild estuary . . . The deep regard in which the wildfowler holds his quarry is such that he will not deliberately fire . . . at any bird . . . which cannot be picked.
From *Modern Wildfowling* by Eric Begbie, 1990

I do not intend to give a discourse on the *anatidae* since they vary tremendously. Some are resident, some are migratory, some are protected, some are legal quarry, some are large, some are small, some are divers, some are dabblers etc. etc. Geese invariably roost on water by night but feed by day while ducks do the complete opposite. However, they all have a lot in common. They are obviously shot, in most cases, over or near water. They are seldom shot in broad daylight but in the half light of dawn and dusk, in pitch darkness or even under a full moon. Like snipe and woodcock, many dogs initially refuse to retrieve wildfowl but, once accustomed to them, cannot retrieve enough of them. A wounded waterfowl in its own element is one of the most difficult of all quarry to retrieve and a wing tipped greylag or Canada goose is a severe physical challenge for *any* dog. Fortunately, however, dead ones generally float! From about nine months old the weight of the dummy should be gradually increased to some 10-12 lb (4.5 - 5 kg) to strengthen the neck and jaw muscles. Lengths of car inner tube filled with weights and sealed, plastic pop bottles filled with enough sand to just give buoyancy stuffed into old shooting stockings with wings attached, etc., etc., are all good practice leading up to 'the real thing'. It will be seen throughout this chapter that, once the all important basic training has been *thoroughly* taught, there is no substitute for practical experience under a sympathetic trainer.

This chapter is more about dogs for wildfowling on the estuary and the foreshore than for duck-shooting (chasing reared mallard off a hole in the ground filled with water) although, obviously, many factors are common to both. At one time any wild brute that could swim was sent wildfowling! Today's wildfowler, however, requires something a little more sophisticated. He requires a large and powerful swimmer with a thick waterproof coat to withstand all weathers. ('The worse the weather, the better the sport' was ever the maxim of the true wildfowler.) His dog must be a 'retrieverholic' yet biddable and merge into its surroundings of dead grass and reeds. Remember that vegetation during the wildfowling season is either dying, dead or very dead! Although a bitch person myself, in general, male dogs make better wildfowling dogs than bitches. It is no coincidence that many of our wildfowling breeds of gundog take their names from the north-eastern seaboard of the United States where the 'waterfowl hunters' and 'market gunners' of the nineteenth century took advantage of the myriads of ducks and geese that they intercepted on their flyways south during their Fall to feed the ever burgeoning cities. We have the Chesapeake Bay retriever, the Nova Scotia Duck Tolling retriever and, of course, the ubiquitous Labrador retriever. The Newfoundland was also originally a 'water dog'. For someone requiring a dog purely for wildfowling I, personally, would rate the 'Chessie' first and the Labrador a close second although a lab is easier to train and more adaptable to other forms of shooting sports as are golden retrievers and flatcoats. Yellow labs need to be as dark coloured as possible and if a springer spaniel (cockers really are too small) must be your choice then choose a large pup with a greater proportion of liver or black because the white bits will certainly show up. Incidentally, a spaniel's coat is not very waterpoof and does not compare with that of a lab or a chessie. I know of several people who use HPRs and a confirmed HPR friend was first attracted to Weimaraners when he saw them being used by numerous wildfowlers along the Baltic coast in mid winter.

Having taught one's pup to swim in still water, it should be introduced to flowing water and the sea itself as soon as possible before it becomes hooked on the easy option of the millpond. Similarly with dummies. Just as the only dummy that any retriever on dry land should actually *see* is its very first one, so the only dummy on *still* water that the 'fowling pupil can actually see should also be its first one. Thereafter, subsequent dummies should be retrieved from flowing water, on the far bank, *beyond* the far bank and so on as the dog's capabilities and experience expand. The Bristol Channel must be full of my dummies! No wildfowling dog should ever be allowed to enter water unless specifically commanded since many is the duck flushed prematurely by a dog rushing ahead to plunge into its favourite element. Steadiness to shot and fall are as important in wildfowling as in driven game shooting. One does not want one's dog retrieving unbidden in case it puts off the next flight of fowl coming in while it is retrieving a bird from the last lot. Never forget that swimming is as physically tiring for a dog as for ourselves.

Take your youngster to the river, throw a marked dummy just onto the far bank and, once the dog has picked it, give the recall whistle and walk downstream encouraging the pupil and manipulating the situation so that the dog emerges from the water at an easy shelving exit. This teaches the pup to use the current to its own advantage rather than to fight it. Always take the retrieve close to the water's edge and, as the pup shakes the water from its coat, command 'SHAKE' in a cart-before-the-horse situation. By continually increasing the distance from the shore one will soon have a dog that shakes the water from its coat *after* delivering the retrieve. This prevents the handler from getting a cold shower and, far more important, prevents the dog from putting down the retrieve to shake which, if winged, will be into the rushes and gone for ever more. It also prevents the dog gripping the duck too hard to prevent it from flying out of its mouth while shaking and thus developing a hard mouth.

One of the wildfowler's most difficult and important tasks is to get his dog to hunt the ground way out *beyond* the far side of the river or pond. (Most dogs will hunt *along* the far bank.) To teach this, put a hidden assistant on the *far* bank and signal them to throw a 'marked' dummy way back from the river. Send the dog with the command 'HI LOST. GET OVER' and when over, 'GET BACK' together with the appropriate handsignals (see chapter on retrieving). Repeat this exercise over several days without either boring or tiring the dog, ensuring that the dummy always lands in roughly the same place until it is 100% reliable at retrieving it. It is then but a short step to place an *unmarked* dummy or 'blind' upwind in exactly the same spot and sending the dog again with exactly the same command. It should go straight to the very spot that had yielded all the previous marked dummies and, 'lo and behold', there is the dummy. Success breeds confidence and, as ever, confidence breeds success. (I once saw a German video in which the dog was towed across the river from a road bridge high above to the exact spot where a live duck with a brailed wing was hidden . . .)

A wildfowling dog has to use its nose in conjunction with its ears rather than its sight more than any other type of retriever so, once it has learned to retrieve by day, give it most of its retrieving lessons at dusk and after dark. It will soon learn to mark the fall of the dummy by sound - and a strong wind will carry a high duck a long way when shot - but, initially, also use the wind direction to help it. One can now buy (non-waterproof) 'dayglo' collars with flashing red lights to keep one informed of the whereabouts of a black lab on a black night! Once a dog is experienced it will soon alert you to the approach of wildfowl, having heard them long before you do, by following their progress with the direction of its head. My old bitch used to give an almost imperceptible whine when duck were approaching and the *only* other time that she ever did that was when I put my bacon rind aside at breakfast!

The most useful training aid of them all for a wildfowling trainer is a bag full of walnut-sized pebbles. Giving a hand signal while simultaneously lobbing a pebble overhand will soon teach the pupil to take directions from the splash and subsequently the hand signal itself – particularly if one is accurate enough to land the pebble alongside the dummy! Remember that, when swimming, a dog's eyes are only just above water level and it will therefore have a very short horizon in choppy water. Pebble throwing requires practice and this should be done *without* the dog present or Fido will become thoroughly confused if the pebble is landing miles away from the dummy! However, once the art of pebble throwing is mastered and a wounded duck is floating down on the current, a well lobbed stone will soon have the dog on the spot. Once the dog has picked up the 'wash' [scent trail on the current], which is probably different from the wind direction, that duck should soon be in the bag. Experience counts for a lot at this game.

When shooting a large lake or loch at evening flight not every bird will be picked that night and a dawn foray is inevitable to complete the pick-up – although one morning I saw an otter that had beaten me to it munching a wigeon! Those dead birds are invariably washed up on the leeward shoreline. (The same thing also occurs on the foreshore but here the tide intervenes.) It is not easy to get a young dog to search exactly where land meets water especially when there are a lot of reeds. However, few dogs can resist boiled liver so cut a boiled liver into sugar lump sized cubes and fasten a dessert spoon on to a long stick. Without the dog being present, walk parallel to the water and place a piece of liver every few yards *exactly* on the shoreline. After, say, 100 yards one can substitute a dummy and, later on, a dead duck at the end of the liver trail. I use a specific word of command 'SEEK SHORE' and before long the pupil is running the exact shoreline until it encounters a proper retrieve. Success on the real thing will hammer this lesson home.

Wounded duck, particularly those of the diving species, take a lot of getting to grips with. As the dog swims towards them they submerge, often for a considerable period of time, before bobbing up again somewhere else. To deal with this common tactic, pass a long nylon line through the ring on a weight and tie a dummy to one end of the line. Throw the weight into the training pond with the line doubled through the ring. Get the dog out of the vehicle and throw the dummy onto the water taking up the slack on the line. Command the dog to retrieve and, as it approaches the dummy, pull on your end of the line and submerge the dummy (see Fig. 6). After some time your assistant, hidden out of sight, slips a second dummy surreptitiously onto the water on your signal while the dog is not looking. The pupil will soon get the message and tread water looking for the quarry to re-appear although the same exercise must eventually be practised in the reeds or other waterside cover where wounded duck will frequently resurface. A few morning flights on the real thing will reinforce this lesson indelibly.

When flighting at dusk on an inland flightpond that has no breeze or current to carry the slain ashore, the usual ploy is to use a powerful torch to show the dog where dead or wounded duck are on the water after the flight. In training sit the dog *behind* and slightly to one side of you in the dark. Switch on the torch and throw the dummy down the beam onto the training pond. Eventually

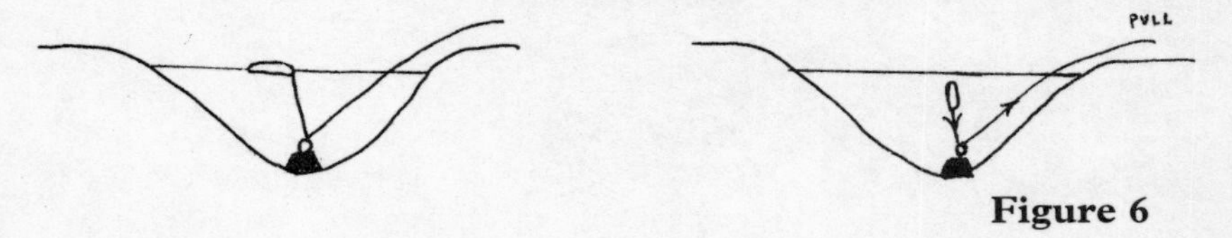

Figure 6

send the dog for the dummy and as soon as it grasps the retrieve, shine the torch on your legs to give it a 'beacon' on which to home back in. Some dogs appear to be particularly obtuse about working with a lamp while others pick it up quite quickly. Again, experience counts.

On the first occasions that you take a youngster out flighting in the dark do not carry a gun yourself and initially stay well back behind the Gun(s). To suddenly shoot right over the head of a young dog in the pitch black dark, however well accustomed to gunfire, is simply asking for trouble. While talking of shooting, always give a wounded bird a second barrel if it is safe to do so (remember that pellets ricochet off water) to make the retrieve simpler.

If using floating decoys try to arrange matters (tide permitting!) to prevent the youngster getting entangled in the anchor lines and make it realise right from the start that decoys are sacrosanct. Few things are more frustrating than having a wounded duck escaping while one's novice is trying to retrieve an anchored plastic decoy! Practice on dry land first. If using a net hide make sure that your dog does not take the whole hide with it in its eagerness to retrieve (see Chapter on Pigeon Shooting) and 'fidgeting' in the hide (scratching, biting twigs, moving around, etc.) should be nipped in the bud at the outset.

Flighting wildfowl can be cold, wet and muddy for both dog and Gun so make life as comfortable for the dog as possible and provide at least a waterproof seat (for the dog!). Without letting it get *fat,* always keep your fowling dog in good condition. Sitting continuously while cold and wet with its energy sapped from 'plowtering' through thick, glutinous mud and swimming against tides and strong currents will soon take its toll – sometimes permanently. You have been warned . . . The solitary coastal wildfowler, like the deerstalker, will form a bond that is missing in more gregarious forms of sport. Above all, your fowling dog will become a great friend and companion on your solitary forays to the estuary and most dogs are generally fairly forgiving when you miss or, even worse, are caught napping!

Pointing grouse in Perthshire.

PLATE 11

No wildfowler should set out with a competent retriever.

PLATE 12

A 'piper' with Richard Chappell behind a 'yacoup' at Slimbridge Duck decoy.

15: Dogs for Woodcock

1 OCTOBER - 31 JANUARY

It takes a good or a lucky man to shoot a right and a left at woodcock but a better or luckier dog to find them both.
Lewis Ibell, beater, Kentchurch Estate, Herefordshire

The woodcock (*scolopax rusticola)* holds a special place in any shooting man's heart to the extent that some landowners will not even have them shot. A magical mystical bird with their unpredictable almost eerie flight, they can be a very testing – or sometimes very easy – shot and the chances of the coveted 'Right and Left' are rare indeed. Of my three chances, two were in the close season and 'I was out with the Missus' on the third!

Like their smaller cousins, the common snipe, woodcock retain a relatively small breeding population in the UK but the majority of woodcock, that bird of myth and legend, come in to our northern and eastern coastlines from Scandinavia and beyond the Arctic Circle on the November full moon, the Hunter's Moon. They, too, need to probe soft ground for invertebrates with their long bills and, as the weather 'hardens' they move south and west to those islands and peninsulas warmed by the Gulf Stream. In an 'open' winter I, personally, do not believe that there are any more of them here but they are merely more spread out over the whole UK land mass. In France it is a highly prized game bird and many French Guns come over expressly to shoot *la bécasse.* (American Guns call it a 'timberdoodle'!) Unfortunately many European woodcock are shot in their breeding grounds in continental Europe by foreign 'sportsmen'.

Woodcock are to be found virtually anywhere. (I recently flushed one with my van when parking on a grass field that would not shelter a fieldmouse!) Apart from the inevitable woodcock shot on a pheasant day there are two types of 'cock shooting for the woodcock *aficionado*. There is woodland shooting and open ground shooting, both of which require different dogs and different tactics.

Take woodland shooting first. This is either carried out in relatively open deciduous woodland consisting of bramble and hazel coppice under oaks or whatever or in brashed conifers when a close working springer or cocker will do well, or is done in those vast conifer plantations so beloved by 'cock where they can lie up by day and rode out to feed in the open fields or on the hill in the gloaming (or the 'dimmity' as they say in the west country). While doe stalking in Sutherland one winter I once counted no less than 34 'cock within half-an-hour as they flighted along the same forestry ride at dusk. Under a holly bush beside a 'window' in the canopy is a favourite place to lie up but they may be found anywhere although they have preferred favourite spots and if you shoot one that spot will often hold another the next time. Incidentally, woodcock will often leg it for a long way in front of advancing beaters before flushing. The Guns usually walk the forestry rides in line astern with one or two 'heading' Guns up front on a cross ride or junction since, once flushed, a woodcock will fly every which way. Meanwhile their dogs work under the thicket on either side. English Springer spaniels, cocker spaniels and the wider ranging Brittany are all grand for this type of work. At ground level in thicket-stage conifers the dogs can move freely but many dogs become 'ride bound' and will not hunt away from the handler to either side of the ride. Indeed, it is one form of shooting where a 'wild' spaniel (and I have known a few!) really comes into its own. We would do well to copy continental or American 'hunters' and fix a proper dog bell to the collar. Not only does it tell us where the dog is but it also moves deer away from the dog in advance which helps to prevent any possible riot. With a pointing dog, 'when the music stops' one can assume that the dog is on point unless, as once happened to me, the bell had come off! My aforementioned excellent American 'bleeper' collar, audible up to 500 yards away, that bleeps every ten seconds when the dog is moving but every second when on point is splendid for this - but it seems a sacrilege to use it, so alien is the noise!

Woodcock are one of the recognised 'nasties' of the retrieving world and, particularly with Brittanies, it is as well to get the retrieving accomplished during training (keep a few in the deep freeze) before teaching the dog to hunt. Woodcock are difficult enough to retrieve by scent but often nearly impossible to retrieve by eye, so good is their camouflage. Until they realise 'the form' many inexperienced dogs will run straight past live or dead woodcock without acknowledging them as a potential quarry. If you have a dog that will not hunt beyond the edge of the ride go back to the boiled liver. I am not an advocate of edible rewards but 'Needs must . . .'. While in training leave the pup in the vehicle and walk along a forestry ride into the wind, 'seeding' either side as far as you can throw the cubes of boiled liver. Get the pup out and encourage it to quarter on either side of the ride for the liver. If you are a woodcock specialist, it is justifiable to run a close-hunting pup alongside a wide ranging hooligan to get it 'out' but this is likely to ruin it for working closer in other types of shooting.

The other form of woodcock 'hunting' is on open ground, hill or marginal land on banks of dead bracken or heather interspersed with whins (gorse), birch and alder scrub wherein they love to lie. Here one requires a wide ranging pointing dog with a lot of white about it or a 'dayglo' collar since in autumn and winter many breeds are extremely well camouflaged when on point. Try spotting an immobile vizsla or Irish setter against dead bracken or a stationary 'pepper-and-salt' German pointer in conifers or on heather that has 'turned'!

Watching an experienced dog winkle a reluctant woodcock out of dead bracken is dogwork at its best. Most pointing dogs will adapt surprisingly easily from grouse to *la bécasse* once a few have been shot over them and woodcock shooting greatly increases their annual working season. With 'bird dogs' you will probably need a retriever as well.

After a day on the woodcock you can be assured that every 'cock in the bag was hard earned by both dog and man. As my friend, woodcock specialist Michael Dawnay, says, 'To appreciate woodcock shooting you must sip your sport not gulp it'.

16: Dogs for Pigeon Shooting

(NO CLOSE SEASON)

Anyone who shoots pigeons without a dog is a blooming fool [or similar words!].
The late Major Archie Coats

The woodpigeon (*columba palumbus*) is the favourite, and in some cases the only, quarry of many sportsmen, and an extremely sporting quarry it is. It may be shot all year round (although many pigeon shooters accord it an unofficial moratorium) and within the space of an hour can present just about every target in the book. Being the only common flying quarry available during the summer months it is an invaluable 'finishing school' for young retrievers destined for game shooting. It is also delicious eating. It is either shot flying in to roost in the woods (mainly during February and March) or decoyed throughout the year over agricultural and market garden crops from newly drilled seed to post harvest stubble as well as early spring clover. It is an attractive object for dogs to retrieve but suffers from one great drawback, *feathers* – those loose, fluffy feathers that many dogs cannot tolerate. It is also frequently shot in extremely hot, cold or scentless conditions and often over very uncomfortable terrain such as rape or other stubble on frozen or bone dry ground.

What of the pigeon shooter's dog? It needs to be a 'retrieverholic' yet be able to sit completely quiet and still for hours when nothing is happening (if you want pigeons to appear, just try filling your pipe or opening a flask!). A dog that blends into the background is an advantage, particularly for roost shooting, but not essential given today's sophisticated camouflaged hides. Size is not an important factor either. However, if pigeon shooting is your main shooting sport I cannot recommend too strongly that you keep that dog *purely* for pigeon shooting for one, if not two, seasons before using it for other jobs. Like flying goshawks at hares, they may retrieve 7, 77 or 777 pigeons before eventually chucking it in for more attractive quarry if introduced to easier alternatives too soon. Dogs do not basically like pigeon feathers. I once lent a small black Labrador bitch called 'Meg' to my friend John Batley for six months. Some 12 years later (but that, as they say, is another story!) he recorded that she had retrieved more than 23,000 pigeons as well as what the late Sir Joseph Nickerson would have described as 'a goodly number of pheasants'! She also taught herself to turn over with her paw any pigeon that fell among the decoys breast upwards! Any of the recognised retrieving breeds are suitable for pigeon shooting with Labradors and English springers being the most popular – but whether that is because they are also used for other forms of shooting or because they are better than any other breed for pigeon shooting I have yet to discover.

It is well worth going to some time and trouble to avoid an aversion to pigeon feathers. Once your pupil is retrieving ordinary dummies, fasten six or eight dried pigeon wings to each dummy with broad elastic bands to give pups the 'feel' of pigeon feathers. When the time eventually comes for cold game insert the dead pigeon in the toe of a discarded pair of tights, secured with a knot.This gives all the advantages of retrieving a pigeon without the disadvantage of the dreaded fluffy feathers and gives the pupil confidence. As always with cold game, make sure that it does not get 'high' and *never* keep using the same old pigeon time after time. When the dog is retrieving these confidently, pluck all the body feathers from the bird until only the head, wings and tail are left feathered. If leisure time is short it may be easier to obtain both pigeons and pigeon wings direct from a gamedealer if there are none in your freezer. Like introduction to gunfire, the feather problem may be imagined rather than real but it is far better to work on the basis that your dog will *not* like them. Eventually the ultimate question must be asked and a fully feathered cold pigeon will be used. A tighter feathered 'cull' racing pigeon is the best retrieve for this exercise and after that, the Real McCoy - a woodpigeon. When the dog's mouth is full of pigeon feathers take care to remove them gently with a forefinger without tweaking its whiskers; if the dog has swallowed too many in the course of a day's shooting, a squirt of cooking oil out of a washing up liquid bottle into its mouth will help to expel them easily as nature intended.

Nothing is more infuriating that to carefully build the ultimate in pigeon shooting hides - and then have the dog charge out to the first bird shot dragging the remains of the hide behind it! Drive four fencing stakes well into the ground on the training field, forming a square of approximately 6 x 6 ft (2 x 2 m). Staple pig netting to three sides of the square from ground level upwards leaving the rear open. Then drape a camouflage net over the front and sides. Sit on a 5 gallon (25 litre) plastic drum within the hide and lob a dummy out to the front. After an interval send the dog. When it has bounced off the pig netting once or twice it will learn to leave via the rear of the hide, re-orient itself and collect the dummy. Some purpose built hides have their own 'dog door' - a sort of cat flap! Talking of re-orienting, I stack small straw bales in three sides of a square, sit on the plastic drum and throw a dummy forward. The dog soon learns to mark by sound, re-orient itself and then retrieve the dummy.

When one has gone to great trouble to lay out a decoy pattern it is infuriating to have ones dog retrieve them all as fast as you put them out! Do not forget that everything that your dog has hitherto retrieved has had your hand scent on it – and that goes for decoys as well. You now want Fido to retrieve the one object that does *not* have any hand scent on it, i.e., your freshly shot pigeon. Get some disposable gloves and shoot a pigeon without the dog present. Pick it up with the glove and put it in a *paper* bag (polythene bags make them sweat).

Stand in a farm gateway with a stockwire fence running away from it with several well-handled pigeons and artificial decoys on, say, the left hand side just out from the fence. Tip your recent 'scentless' pigeon out of the paper bag on the right hand side of the fence. Get the dog out of the vehicle, sit it in the gateway and send it down the right hand side of the fence. With 'NOs' and 'GOOD DOGS' as appropriate it should eventually retrieve the 'scentless' pigeon while ignoring the decoys and well handled pigeons just on the other side of the stock fence (which it can obviously both see and smell). The next step is to spread a few well-handled pigeons and decoys in a wide semi-circle and fasten them securely to the ground. Tip another 'scentless' pigeon in the centre and slightly your side of the semi-circle, fetch the dog and eventually send it to retrieve. Again with appropriate 'NOs' and 'GOOD DOGS' it should get the message. Some dogs pick this lesson up more quickly than others.

Remember that gunfire in a hide is at extremely close quarters and the youngster has probably not seen the quarry anyway so make sure that the dog has been well introduced to gunfire before taking it pigeon shooting - and then be somewhat tactful about it.

When spending hour after hour in a pigeon hide with frequently little or nothing happening, like the wildfowler or deerstalker, you will form a very close bond with your dog. Every pigeon shooting *aficionado* who regularly shoots over a dog will tell you that there is no way that they would ever shoot pigeons without one.

17: Dogs for Deerstalking

Seasons for the species and sexes of deer in England, Wales and Scotland all differ

No one should ever shoot roe without some well-trained dog to follow them when wounded as no other animal is more often lost when mortally wounded.
Wild Sports and Natural History of the Highlands by Charles St. John, 1848

I have repeatedly stressed that some dogs, like humans, are better than others for a particular job. Never is this more so than with deerstalking. Some individuals take to it straightaway while a litter brother or sister my have little or no interest in deer work at all. There are two main tasks for a deer dog. The first is to indicate possible cull animals, i.e. unshot deer, to the stalker and the second is to follow up dead or wounded deer and then indicate their whereabouts to the stalker. This chapter sets out the basic principles of training a deer dog but you will have to work out what suits you and your dog best for your deer species and type of country to achieve the desired result. Over the years you will both form an extremely effective partnership but your next dog may be completely different from its predecessor and you may have to try completely different methods to achieve the same ultimate result.

A dog is also an excellent silent companion in what is essentially a solitary occupation and the stalker will establish a rapport with their dog that is seldom found in other shooting sports except perhaps wildfowling. Those professional deer managers who take out foreign clients will be expected to have a trained deer dog – even if only to rectify the client's mistakes! In Germany, Norway, Denmark, Poland and, I believe, Austria it is illegal to stalk without a trained dog and in Sweden, if one does not own a trained dog, one must, by law, arrange to have one at 60 minutes call before setting out.

To the uninitiated, one stalks deer into the wind so that their incredibly sensitive noses cannot detect the stalker's presence. At the same time the scent of the deer is being blown back to the dog that stays permanently beside the stalker. The other important thing to realise about deer is that, particularly if they are suspicious prior to the shot, a deer shot straight through the heart can run up to 150 yards (140 metres) before dropping and, in layman's terms, is clinically stone dead while running. This is called the 'flight reflex.' In thick cover or in poor light the carcase will obviously take some finding by human eye.

What of the dogs? Just about every conceivable breed of dog has been used for following up dead or wounded deer but today's stalker wants a dog that will stalk beside him rather than some mutt left in the vehicle until a crisis has occurred. The four attributes of any deer dog are:

1. A good nose for both ground and air scent.
2. The ability to remain sitting or at heel almost indefinitely.
3. 'Trainability.'
4. An aptitude for deer work. This can obviously only be assessed once the dog has started training. Fortunately, nine out of ten dogs take to deer work to some degree since deer are a natural canine prey species.

Colour is important. A dark or neutral colour is a must and avoid more than a minimal amount of white like the plague. I have known several light-coloured stalking dogs that stood out so much they had to wear a camouflage jacket! Equally I have had solid liver dogs out stalking that have moved and caused deer to look in their direction and then carry on grazing. (I can only assume that they took the dog for another deer!) Stalking is another sport where a good big'un will always beat a good littl'un, particularly with the larger species of deer.

Although individuals vary in ability, some breeds are more likely to produce the attributes of a good deer dog than others. Before going on to the gundogs there are many other breeds that potentially make excellent deer dogs. Some of these are:

Alsatian (German Shepherd Dog) Probably the ultimate deer dog because they have brains as well! Consider what the police train them for and then apply the same *criteria* to deer work. The problem is finding one that is physically and mentally sound.

Border collie ('Sheepdog') Intelligent, very trainable, good noses, will bark easily but many are inherently gunshy. I know of more than one that has learned to round up roe deer in blocks of forestry to its owner who is waiting in armed ambush! Collie x sighthound lurchers are frequently too keen on chasing unshot deer once they know what it is all about.

Terriers (Borders, Jack Russells etc.) Having owned and still own Jack Russells I have always maintained that 'A trained terrier is a contradiction in terms and Jack Russells are things that you give to people you don't like!' They are small enough to take up into a high seat, will usually bay a carcass but they suffer from the 'hound mentality' i.e. they work for themselves rather than their owner and, once their nose is down on a scent, their ears become completely blocked! Keep them purely for deer work and certainly do not enter them to ground. I have trained some very effective Border terriers for deer work.

'Teckels' (working bred dachshunds originating from Germany) These, too, suffer from the 'the hound mentality', and, although natural blood trailers, tracking is only a small part of their repertoire on the continent, some of their other tasks being working to fox or badger below ground, beating, locating and driving unshot quarry while *unaccompanied* and retrieving ducks off water! Black and tan, they come in smooth-, broken- and long-coated varieties. Teckels suffer from the pups being so 'cute and cuddly' that their owners 'feel sorry for them'. *Don't*! Regard them as miniature rottweilers right from day one! Many teckels are fine during training but, once they realise what the job is all about, they reckon that they know more about it than the Boss and 'make their own arrangements' if not kept under the thumb! Most will 'speak' on a blood trail and/or on finding a dead or, more particularly, wounded beast.

No teckel, or for that matter, terrier destined for deerstalking should *ever* be allowed free running exercise outside a teckel/terrier proof (almost a contradiction in terms itself!) garden throughout its life. Once they learn to hunt for themselves, let alone going to ground, their stalking role is immediately compromised and they become a confounded liability.

Bavarian and Hanoverian Mountain Bloodhounds (Bayrischer Gebirgschweisshund) These are russet-coloured specialist tracking dogs and are reputed to follow a five-day-old blood trail under good scenting conditions but that should never be necessary in Britain. They also suffer from 'the hound mentality' although to a lesser extent. When properly trained, however, they can be extremely good deer dogs.

To enjoy ones stalking with the 'hound mentality' breeds the best way to stalk and relax at the same time is with a leather (or cord) loop over the right shoulder to the left hip (for right-handed shots) which then runs as a single line to a clip on the dog's collar. Then both hands are permanently free and the dog is permanently at heel. I, personally, have never had a problem when stalking with any of the above breeds through 'game rich ground' *off* the lead but (a) the basic training has been 200% sound and (b) they have not had many deer shot over them. Incidentally, no terrier-sized dog should ever stalk with *just* a collar on because, should it goes to ground with one on, it will eventually get caught up in an underground root and the dog will end up dead.

We now come to the gundog breeds which fall into four groups or categories.

Pointers and Setters Bred to gallop over large stretches of open ground, they are purely air scenters and not really suitable for stalking. Pointers and English setters are also mainly white in colour.

Spaniels For which read working bred English springers and cockers (although field spaniels have been exported to Scandinavia for work on bears; their British breeders assuring me it is because they are too stupid to realise the ultimate consequences!). Although several professional stalkers use them, English springers usually have too much white on them for deer work, the tail never stops wagging and they are happiest when on the move rather than staying permanently beside the stalker. I once had an Austrian chamois hunter come to me for a replacement springer pup but the litter all had too much white on them. Bar many cockers being a more suitable colour for stalking, the same problems also apply to them. Spaniels are not really a great choice for a deer dog.

Retrievers Until recently probably more deer were shot over black Labradors than all the other breeds put together. Golden retrievers and flat-coats have also been used successfully and I am sure that 'Chessies' would make admirable deer dogs. They all walk to heel and sit indefinitely, will indicate unshot deer and are good blood trailers. However it is very difficult to get working bred retrievers to give tongue (although this problem can be overcome) and many are too gentle to 'mix it' with a wounded beast. The problem with labs is that no-one has ever bred a line of stalking Labradors and, however good their antecedents may be on winged game, there is no guarantee that they will take to deer work. The best labs seem to be Scottish bred male dogs (although many have shortened working lives from running behind quad bikes from puppyhood!). Retrievers also frequently suit their owner's game shooting requirements. With some hesitation, I would consider using a working bred lab with a strong dash of show blood if purely meant for deer work which gives it a bit of 'the hooligan' that is sometimes necessary.

HPRs Although something of an acquired taste, most HPR breeds have been selectively bred on the continent for work on deer and boar for many generations. They will walk to heel indefinitely, point deer, give tongue (extremely easily!), will tackle a wounded beast and they are extremely deer orientated. The four German HPRs (GSP, GWP, Weimaraner and Large Munsterlander)and the Hungarian vizsla are particularly suited to deer work while the Brittany is not really suitable being very spaniel-like; I have no experience of the two Italian breeds for stalking.

For deer work a male dog is preferable to a bitch. Apart from 'heat' which is less of a problem here anyway, a male dog is more persevering on a difficult blood trail, has more killer instinct and more weight to throw into the argument with a wounded beast than a bitch. Choice of breed may well be dictated by the terrain and the species of deer stalked as well as ones other shooting sports. In the northern half of Britain a dog with a protective coat is preferable to a thin-skinned breed. There is no reason why the same dog cannot be used for game shooting as well as stalking but, apart from dummy work at that receptive age, confine it to deer work for a full twelve months before introducing it to game shooting. Do *not* do it the other way round and certainly do not try to teach it to do both jobs at once. Incidentally it will be a lot steadier when it gets on to game and, while stalking, if it shows an interest in other game do be tactful. If you have numerous deer on your doorstep ensure that your pup does not get into the habit of chasing them. Should it happen, stay where you are and keep whistling. The pup will eventually return when you grit you teeth, smile sweetly and pretend that it never happened. Merely ignore it but make sure that it does not happen a second time. Do not take the pup with you in the vehicle when stalking or you will ask it to run before it can walk and if you have 'a portable high seat with wing mirrors' you will deafen it and make it gunshy to boot!

From about 16-20 weeks old a deer dog should realise that its place in life is at heel although it should be allowed a daily gallop in the play/exercise area to let off steam. When you eventually take it stalking (particularly before dawn) ensure that it does not gallop off and 'clear the wood' as soon as it is released from the vehicle! Deer dogs should have very little exercise throughout their lives as the work is not demanding and a very fit deer dog or, worse, one that has learned to hunt is a confounded nuisance.

COMMANDS

Not many to worry about: a low hiss and/or the flat of the hand in front of the dog's face for SIT, patting one's thigh for HEEL. At first this is greatly exaggerated but gradually reduced to merely tapping the seam of one's trousers with a forefinger. (In training one initially uses the verbal command 'HEEL' in conjunction with tapping one's thigh but can dispense with the command as soon as the lesson is learned.) To get the dog to go DOWN put the flat of the hand on the dog's head and to place the dog *behind* you so that you are not both competing for the same narrow ride put your hand in front of its nose and push gently rearwards. Apart from laying the dog on a blood trail, that is it!

THE DROP

Having frequently stressed that the *basic training* is all important in all gundog work, never is that more so than with deer work. Get the basics 110% right first. One of the very first stalkers I ever met with a dog was a Scottish stalker who maintained that he 'gave the beggar a bit of deer liver and he's been a grand stalking dog ever since' – but refused to believe that anyone could stalk with a dog at heel off the lead!

Having thoroughly taught the Drop while you *walk* away (see Chapter 7, Basic Training) the next step is to teach the Drop while you *crawl* away, a lesson that will have many practical applications in the field.

To teach the dog to crawl beside one is not difficult. Sit the dog and lie down beside it. Hiss it down and crawl forward calling the dog beside you with your hand patting down on its back. With a combination of hissing, 'DOWN' and 'HEEL' most dogs get the message fairly easily. To call the dog to you on its belly use a combination of 'HERE' and 'DOWN'.

To teach a dog to sit below a high seat (terriers and teckels fit nicely in a roe sack up aloft!) you will need to lean a 10-12 ft (3-3.6 m) domestic ladder against a tree (or telegraph pole!). Dig the feet into the ground and secure the top of the ladder to the tree – I speak from experience! Tie a rope with a metal ring attached round the tree about 3 ft (90 cm) above ground level. Pass a long line, similar to an extended slip lead, through the ring and round the dog's neck. With the other end of the line in your hand so that it is slightly slack slowly ascend the ladder ensuring that the dog watches you ascend. (They often panic if they suddenly cannot see you.) Should it move you can sharply jerk the line to remind it that you are still in charge. A child's water pistol in your other hand should forestall any whining! When in the field a familiar article of clothing laid beside the dog below the high seat will give it confidence and anchor it.

HEEL

A deer dog spends 99% of its time at heel so get it right. A deer dog should walk three-quarter length in front of the stalker with its quarters level with the stalker's leg (on the left side for a right-handed rifle and *vice versa*). The reasons for walking three-quarter length in front are, first, the stalker will notice the dog pointing deer and, secondly, the dog has the advantage of every eddy of breeze without it being foiled by the 'blud 'n' mud' on the stalker's boots. Most dogs will draw slightly forward into the wind and hang back slightly when going downwind but make sure that that three-quarter length *stays* at three-quarter length and does not become a length and then two lengths and so on (the reason for stalkers carrying a long stick!). If the dog naturally hangs back in 'Labrador mode' either hold a thumbstick horizontal to the ground pointing forward with the slip lead passed through the vee and keep pushing the dog forward or bring a light switch in your right hand round behind you and keep tapping the dog's hocks from behind to push it forward. The dog should walk with its head permanently up so that it can wind deer at the maximum distance and not get involved with the footscent of other game or deer. (Footscent is always taboo.) Any attempt to put its head to the ground ('hunting at heel') should be thwarted by tapping it under the chin with ones toe or putting the slip lead on just behind the ears and giving a sharp upward jerk *every* time it transgresses. The 'hound mentality' brigade cannot help walking *nez à terre* and I have long given up trying to raise their heads when at heel!

It is vitally important to make sure that the dog's head is to the rear of the rifle muzzle when taking a shot if you wish to preserve its hearing. Hissing the dog into sitting position prior to firing will automatically bring its head further to the rear.

INDICATING UNSHOT DEER

Although a deer dog may be called upon to find a dead or wounded deer very rarely, it is working 60 minutes in the hour all the time it is out in its pointing role. Many dogs will point deer having had a few killed over them but they will also point squirrels, rabbits, pheasants etc. in the process. By teaching them to point deer in a deer park, on a deer farm or even on ones own 'patch' while in training one can eliminate much of the 'riot' element. Dogs will also *see* deer through the trees at their eye level. Do not forget that the wind strength and direction at the dog's (and the couched deer's level) may be very different from that at the stalker's face level, especially in a valley-type situation. Teaching a dog to point deer is exactly the same as teaching a dog to point any other game (see Chapter 10, Pointing). For some years I used a bottle-reared muntjac that was reared on the lawn by the kennels for teaching this lesson. When transferred to his adult enclosure he had a *penchant* for trotting over during this lesson and licking the trainee's nose!

When out stalking 'in anger' and the young dog goes on point it may be pointing a deer or herd of deer that is actually there, pointing the 'haunt' where deer no longer are, i.e., have slipped away, pointing a deer and the wind has veered or backed so it can no longer scent it, pointing a squirrel or even a far off sheep. Do not be in too much of a hurry to praise the dog. Wait until you see the end result of the point. It is all part of the dog's learning curve. A single deer at close quarters or a herd much further off will initially get the same response but eventually you will get to read that dog like a book, if you have the wit to do so, and its body language will tell you a lot, such as which species it is indicating in a multi-species area. When 'roding in' on deer always give the dog the benefit of the doubt if no deer are actually forthcoming for the reasons just given. Quietly clicking your fingers in front of its nose will usually get the dog roding in and I have often had novice dogs take me up to 150 yd (140 m) to where deer were lying up.

Do not let a good 'deer indicator' make you an idle stalker! Any dog will only know whatever its nose tells it and it is only an adjunct to your binoculars...!

BLOOD TRAILING

Having established that a heart shot deer will often run up to 150 yd (140 m) while apparently 'stone dead', it must then be found which is often difficult for humans, particularly in bad light or thick cover. This is no more difficult for most dogs, though, than following a 'winged' pheasant if it is taught correctly. One can deduce from the 'pins' and 'paint' [hairs and blood] and the reaction to the shot where on the body the deer was hit and what it is likely to do but one still has to actually find the blooming thing! The term 'blood trail' is actually something of a misnomer. Initially the dog is almost certainly following the 'sweat scent', 'fear scent' or 'adrenalin scent' that appears to be extremely strong for some minutes or hours after the shot but this soon evaporates while the actual blood scent can still be followed for up to several days thereafter. It is essential that the dog is trained on *cold* blood. To train it on freshly shot deer in the field and then expect it to follow up a blood trail the following morning – why is it that only clients make mistakes – is akin to training a retriever on warm pheasants and then expecting it to retrieve canvas dummies?

My stalking mentor (a Matabele tracker called Patrick) insisted that after the shot we smoked a cigarette (one of mine!) to give the bullet time to do its work through shock, tissue damage and blood loss – if the kudu or impala was dead, it was not going anywhere anyway. The sound of the shot itself seldom upsets game but people or dogs charging about after a mortally wounded animal most certainly does and the beast will get up and go for a considerable distance purely on adrenalin, making the subsequent follow-up a lot more difficult. Blood trailing lessons can be taught from any age and 16 weeks is not too early but, like dummies for retriever puppies, should be seen as a privilege and a pleasure rather than a chore. Once a fortnight is plenty and then only in good scenting conditions, that is, avoiding extremes of wind, heat, cold or wet.

First, as Mrs Beeton may have said, obtain your blood. When you or a friend go stalking collect the blood in two polythene freezer bags placed one inside the other with a dessertspoon of table salt mixed in to prevent the blood congealing into a jelly. Label it and put it in the freezer until required. My freezer once broke down and I obtained sheep's blood from the abattoir which did the job but I am convinced that the blood of one deer species smells completely different from the blood of another species, so freeze the blood of as many deer species as you can and introduce them relatively early on. Do not get the dog hooked on one species and averse to others which is easy to do. When the dog is confidently following blood trails it is time to lay a trail of a deer's stomach contents (with a small amount of blood added) for the time when your dog has to track a gutshot beast – yes, we all do it – and no actual blood is forthcoming. Ensure that your blood, deer offal, deer head or whatever is not 'high' or you are merely teaching the dog to hunt carrion.

There are two Golden Rules for laying blood trails:

1 Lay the trail *downwind*. This means that the scent is being blown away from the dog and it has to put its nose to the ground to follow it. (Many dogs, particularly the pointing breeds, will try to 'air scent' the carcase and, since one stalks deer into the wind, they will usually run either into or across the wind when mortally wounded which encourages this undesirable habit. It wastes a lot of time and disturbs other deer.)

2 The foot scent and the blood scent should be kept separate. This is best achieved by tying some string to a long stick (like a fishing rod and line) to which the blood-soaked flannel/towel is attached. Hold the stick at right angles so the trail is parallel to your footsteps. This method enables the trail to be 'broken' or changes in direction made.

Initially the blood trail should be short, straight and continuous. As the dog gains confidence and experience the trail can be made longer, 'broken' and with changes in direction to make it more difficul. The beginning and end of the trail, as well as changes in direction should be marked. Branches broken out of the hedge do well. If the markers are too obvious a 'fly' dog will soon gallop straight to the end marker for the reward! The blood trail should first be laid on a stock free grass field and then in light cover such as bracken or long grass and so on to the edge of woodland rides. (I once saw an article on blood trailing in a Swedish magazine which showed the trainer tying three blood-soaked sponges to his rear bicycle wheel and then pedalling along a forestry track!) On the continent novice dogs have to follow only ½ litre of blood laid over 500 m 12 hours beforehand and advanced dogs have to follow ½ litre laid over 1,000 m 24 hours earlier - and that is the 'bog standard' test! Blood trailing is one of the very few lessons where I use an edible reward - usually tripe. This not only encourages the dog to follow the trail but, in the later stages, also tells it that it has got to the end of the trail and it does not cast forward seeking the next drop of blood which no longer exists. Edible rewards are best used in conjunction with air dried deer skins or fresh carcasses hidden at the end of the blood trail. When blood trailing always use the same command 'SEEK' or 'WHERE'S THE DEER' which *only* applies to blood trailing and put a specific collar or harness on the dog prior to tracking.

Putting on the collar triggers 'blood trailing' in the dog's mind.

A line can be attached to the collar (do not use a slip lead) to steer the dog back onto the blood trail during training.

Bells or transmitters can be attached to the collar.

Lay one or more blood trails wearing rubber kitchen gloves while the dog is out of sight in the car or kennel – you can only run a dog over each blood trail once so lay several while you are at it. Having got to the end marker flip the blood rag over and retrace your steps as accurately as you can back to the start thus doubling the strength of the trail. One is trying to make it as easy as possible for the pup at this stage. Remove the gloves, then put the tracking collar or harness and line on the dog. Take it to the start of the blood trail holding the line, crouch or kneel down to prevent the dog looking up at you and click your fingers over the trail (hence the rubber gloves – if you hands are covered in blood the dog will concentrate on your hands) and say 'WHERE'S THE DEER'. The dog may show interest (a few tiny morsels of tripe along the first few yards of the blood trail helps), may look at you, may look completely clueless, etc., etc. In continental Blood Trailing Competitions the judges allow a dog up to 15 minutes to get 'tuned in' to the scenting conditions so be in no hurry. If the dog dwells on the start point indefinitely you must put some forward pressure on the collar via the line to make the dog realise that it is a *linear* exercise. As the dog follows the trail quietly tell it 'GOOD DOG. WHERE'S THE DEER' without distracting it as long as it is on the trail. (If the wind has shifted since laying the trail it may have drifted the blood scent parallel to the actual visible trail.) If the dog veers off the trail altogether *keep quiet* and, with the line, draw it gently but firmly back onto the trail when you can continue praising it again. Progress at *the dog's pace* and not at your own. When the dog eventually reaches the tripe make an enormous fuss of it. Some dogs, as ever, are slower than others to get the message but keep trying without overfacing the dog and most get there in the end since most dogs actually enjoy blood trailing. The most common faults are teaching it in bad scenting conditions, using too little blood in the early stages, distracting the dog by talking too volubly or allowing something extraneous to distract it. If you have no luck initially do not 'flog a dead horse' but leave it entirely alone for a fortnight or more and try it somewhere else when all should then go well.

You are stalking 'in anger'. At dusk you have heart shot a beast in a conifer plantation and laid on your trusty hound. You now have a black dog in a black wood on a black night that is quite capable of finding your deer but how do you know where they both are? If the method that suits the pair of you involves making a noise, then so be it, even if it 'clears the wood'. Your *first* priority is to find that beast by whatever means.

The 'Halving' Method

This involves giving the dog time to find the carcase then whistling it back to you (some dogs will return of their own accord), examining its muzzle for deer 'pins' or 'paint' if it 'mouths' the carcase and again commanding 'WHERE'S THE DEER'. Each time you follow the dog as far as you can until you lose sight of it and keep repeating the process until you come across the carcase. In the early days whenever you shoot a deer, sit the dog beside it, back off, call the dog to you, SAY 'WHERE'S THE DEER' and let it run back to the carcass. Play all the variations of returning to the dog beside the deer and so on giving lavish praise every time the dog gets it right. Many stalkers have stalked for years using nothing more sophisticated!

Speaking to the Line

This involves the dog 'speaking' [barking] like a foxhound along the blood trail and is mainly inherited. Some GSPs (which have a lot of foxhound in their original make up), teckels and mountain bloodhounds will do it. The best tutor is the pup's dam if she already does it but many pet beagles will set an example if you can borrow one and the pack instinct may well take over.

With a naturally mute dog such as a working bred Labrador one can resort to artificial means and attach a pair of goshawk bells as used in falconry to the collar. These can be heard up to half a mile away if your hearing is not deaf to that decibel range. When not in use a strip of cloth or leather inserted through the slit in each bell and bound with sellotape will keep them quiet. Going more hi-tech, the Americans (who else?) have invented a collar-mounted transmitter which operates at the same frequency as the hawk's transmitter and the receiver will pick up a directional signal over several miles. I am importing some American 'bleeper' collars for pointers that emit a piercing whistle every 10 seconds when the dog is moving and every second when motionless on point. Even *I* can hear it at over 500 yards! Any of these need to be introduced when the dog is confidently following blood trails whilst still in training rather than waiting until you have a 'runner' on your hands in the field.

'Shall I, shan't I?' A floating dummy upwind and just out of reach of this GSP.

PLATE 13

The author about to cast off a young pointer.

A drop is the kingpin of training: a GSP demonstrates.

PLATE 14

Teaching a well-bred 'English' pointer pup to drop by merely growling at it.

Speaking to a Dead or Wounded Deer

This lesson is easier to teach than speaking to a blood trail, particularly with naturally vociferous dogs. Unfortunately, naturally vociferous dogs also tend to be naturally vociferous in kennels and great tact is required to encourage wanted noise but to discourage unwanted noise! The continentals set great store by the *Totverbeller* (or dog that sits beside the carcase and barks indefinitely) and it certainly saves a lot of time in recovery. The difficult bit is to get the dog to bark to command in the first place after which one can adapt the lesson to any given situation - obviously in this case deer. There are four methods of achieving this:

The Police Method At feeding time attach the dog to a strong point by a line clipped to its collar and bate it with its main meal just out of reach. When it barks out of frustration command 'BARK' or 'SPEAK' (similar to 'SEEK') and reward it with its food and praise. Alternatively place the food on the other side of the kennel door. Repeat this every night until you can get it to bark to command before producing its main meal.

The German (soft) Method Similar to the above but the dog is shown its main meal which is then covered with an air dried deer skin topped with a rag soaked in deer blood to give the scent association and the dog commanded to eat. It scratches at the deer skin to get at the food underneath and when it barks out of frustration the skin is whipped away and again the command 'BARK' or 'SPEAK' is given as the food is uncovered. Again, this is repeated nightly until the required result is obtained.

The Gambrel Method When you shoot a deer – and a muntjac doe makes a better subject than a red stag – haul the carcass up a tree with a gambrel and pulley and juggle it up and down just out of reach of the dog while whooping and hollering, barking and generally revving the dog up. When it barks command 'BARK' and lower the carcass and reward the dog with some gralloch. Repeat this every time you shoot a deer until the message gets through. A word of warning – make sure that no-one is watching this performance or you may get carted away to an institution by men in white coats!

The Continental Method This might not find universal favour here since it is similar to 'force retrieving' i.e. the infliction of discomfort until the dog does as required when the discomfort ceases but the *Totverbeller* is highly thought of in Germany. It requires a mentally tough 'hooligan' which is tied up tightly to two strong points on either side of the collar so that it cannot move its head far. It is then lightly attacked with a stick until it barks when the attacking stops and it is praised. The principle is that as long as it barks it is being praised but as soon as it stops it is attacked until it starts barking again. This lesson is taught daily until it will bark for 30-40 minutes without stopping. The dog is then sat behind a deer carcass and taught to bark without attempting to mouth the deer.

Having taught the dog to bark to command this then has to be applied to an air dried deer skin, then a cold carcass and then to the real thing as well as ensuring that the dog stays with the beast but does not try to eat it!

You must work out which of all the above methods suits you and your dog and, whichever you decide upon, it will take time and commitment to reach the required end but, as long as it produces the goods, the method matters not at all.

THE BRINGSEL TECHNIQUE

The *bringsel* technique was developed for when the 'quarry' was too big to be physically retrieved by the dog. The dog found the quarry and then returned to the handler with a *bringsel* or leather strap in its mouth to inform the handler that the quarry had been found and then led him back to the quarry. It was originally developed by the German Army during World War I for Alsatians to go into No-Man's-Land after dark to find wounded soldiers, return to the handler who would then lead out the stretcher party to bring them in. It was subsequently evolved for mountain and avalanche rescue and only relatively recently for deer work. Training a dog for the *bringsel* technique takes me at least six weeks and at some point the dog usually has a 'hiccup'. Make haste slowly . . .

The basic training technique is as follows:

1. Teach the dog to retrieve the *bringsel* like an ordinary dummy.
2. Peg down an air-dried deer skin in the open and place the *bringsel* on top. Send the dog for the *bringsel* with the double word of command 'WHERE'S THE DEER. SEEK'. With a combination of 'NOs' and 'GOOD DOGs' or whatever insist on it retrieving the *bringsel* and *not* the skin. On its return with the *bringsel* command 'WHERE'S THE DEER' and return to the skin with the dog and relieve it of the *bringsel beside the skin* with much praise. Always take the *bringsel* from the dog beside the skin or carcass.
3. Lay a blood trail (which the dog is already proficient at following) into light cover where the skin is hidden with the *bringsel* on it. Repeat as in lesson 2
4. Lay a blood trail with the skin hidden as before but tie the *bringsel* to the dog's collar with a 10 in. (25 cm) cord. Send the dog with 'WHERE'S THE DEER. SEEK'. On encountering the skin the dog should pick up the *bringsel* in its mouth and return. Continue as in lesson 2.
5. Remove the cord and attach the *bringsel* direct to its collar and proceed as in Lesson 4.

When you eventually shoot a deer over the dog, leave the dog on the drop and go forward to check that the beast is dead before returning and sending the dog. Monitor the first few deer to ensure that the drill is correctly followed and that the dog is not too carried away by the carcass. A potential snag arises when the deer is only wounded and as soon as the dog returns, the deer breaks its bay and takes off again.

TAKING A NOVICE DOG OUT IN THE FIELD

Having spent a considerable amount of time and effort in getting your dog this far it would be sheer folly to ruin it all for the sake of a few stalking outings. Like any other form of gundog work, training does not stop one day and work start the next but the dog is still being trained for the whole of its first season and, indeed, for the rest of its working life. Therefore on your first few outing do not load your rifle with ammunition thus ensuring that you are still a dog trainer rather than a stalker! Any faults that start to creep in must be quickly and firmly nipped in the bud or you will forever regret it since they will only get worse. If it means raising your voice or even giving the dog 'what for' then do so. Some faults to watch out for are:

Hunting at heel (walking with its nose on the ground).

'Pulling' beyond the three-quarter length ahead of you.

Pointing or acknowledging game other than deer - be tactful if it is destined to go game shooting later and remember that grey squirrels seem to smell like fallow deer.

'Fidgeting' on the drop, i.e. chewing twigs, scratching etc.

Barking or whining at unshot deer.

Chasing unshot deer.

Evenings are best for the first few outings since the dog will have all day in which to let off steam before creeping along at ¼ mile an hour. Young dogs lose concentration after a couple of hours so, instead of continually nagging at it, retire it to the vehicle and continue without it until you shoot something.

When you eventually shoot a deer make sure that the dog is relaxed before firing. If you whistle immediately before taking a heart shot the deer, although dead, will often take off for some distance before dropping thus ensuring a blood trail. Note the dog's reaction to the first full bore rifle fired at very close quarters. Reassure the dog. Wait for five full minutes before walking the dog in to the 'strike' *at heel* now and forever afterwards. *Always* send the dog from the 'strike' and never from the firing position. When you reach the carcase take time to make an enormous fuss of the dog and make it understand that a dead deer is the most important thing in the world to both of you. Note how it reacts to its first dead deer - some can be very disappointing. Cut the throat and encourage it to take an interest in that part of the deer's anatomy. Many dogs will do anything from licking the bullet hole to actually eating the carcase. Some will be terrified of the dead animal while others will show no interest whatsoever. Use a bit of tact with the first few deer and thereafter only allow them to 'rag' the head and neck. If the dog starts getting over-eager at the shot, fire into the ground beside a deer that is out of season or outside the cull plan and walk off with the dog at heel in the opposite direction. It is extremely important that, after the first few deer, you only blood trail the dog on deer that it has to actually work for. Blood trailing a dog 15 yards on a grass field to a carcase that it can already see is similar to asking a retriever to pick up pheasants lying dead on the grass 15 yards from your peg! It bores them rigid and makes them unsteady. Keep them both for the difficult ones and you will keep them finely tuned.

On the first occasion I allow the dog to 'assist' with the gralloch but thereafter the dog should sit close by. Watch the dog to make sure that it does not slip off after the rest of the herd or take off hunting while you are engrossed. When it eventually has to tackle a wounded deer, whatever your own thoughts on the matter, the dog will have to make its own arrangements since it will probably be some way away from you. If that method succeeds it is likely to use the same method ever afterwards. *Ensure that the dog is out of the way* if you have to give a wounded deer the *coup de grâce*. I know of at least two stalkers who did not with disastrous results.

When dragging a carcass make sure that the dog walks to heel. Dragging a 70 lb (30 kg) carcass is bad enough without an additional 70 lb dog hanging on to it!

MOVING DEER

When moving (a quieter form of driving) deer to waiting rifles make sure the dog remains to heel. On no account be tempted to use it as a 'spaniel for deer' or you will always regret it. Since moving is invariably done downwind the mere scent of the dog and a metallic rattle (falconry bells are excellent for this) should get the deer afoot and moving quietly forward.

CONCLUSION

Having a trained deer dog will add a completely new dimension to your stalking and, although you will initially lose deer through the dog moving, being clumsy etc., you will sooner or later greatly increase your chances of achieving your cull targets. You will have more opportunities for a shot and having a reliable dog will give you the confidence to take shots that are within your capability but that you would have turned down before i.e. shots at last light. The extra venison revenue will more that cover the cost of keeping the dog (how many other Guns can say that!), he will become a valued friend and stalking companion and, once you have stalked with a good dog, you would never ever contemplate stalking without one.

18: Gundogs for Falconry

Good dogs make good hawks. Anon.

The Good Lord may not have got everything right, but one thing He did get right was that He gave hawks the summer in which to moult in order that falconers should have the time to train their dogs! Successful falconry has sometimes been described as a 'three-legged stool' requiring a sound falconer, a sound hawk and a sound dog in order to remain upright! Because the dog is invariably a second class citizen compared with one's hawk it is essential to train it thoroughly while one has the chance because, in my experience, once the hawk is taken up all further dog training usually ceases forthwith! For anyone wishing to train a dog for falconry all of the foregoing general chapters, with the obvious exception of Retrieving, apply equally to falconry dogs. (Incidentally, never turn down a dog for falconry because it retrieves. Dogs are not so stupid that they do not know whether they are hawking or shooting. Prior to the use of freezers in private homes, everything our hawks ate was caught, run over on the road or shot and we used our dogs to retrieve whatever was shot for hawk food. By the same token, there is no reason why one should not use the same dog for both shooting and falconry.)

Prior to about 1960 things were simple. Game and lark hawkers flew their falcons over pointers or (mainly) English setters and austringers flew their goshawks over spaniels - and that was it (with the exception of sparviters and rook hawkers who never used a dog anyway). After that time three factors changed the whole falconry scenario for ever. First, redtails and later Harris hawks began to be imported in large numbers, coupled with the captive breeding of British and imported birds of prey followed by hybrids of all origins. Secondly, the interest in practical falconry – due largely to the arrival of the Harris' hawk – increased phenomenally from some 40 of us then to some 4,000 actual falconers out of some 13,000 licensed raptor keepers in the 1990s and, thirdly, the continental Hunter Pointer Retrievers started arriving in Britain from BAOR via returning ex-Servicemen which greatly increased the choice of breed for all branches of falconry.

If a person takes up falconry or a falconer moves to a new area they would be wise to discover what the terrain and cover are like and what quarry species the area holds before deciding upon what type of hawk to acquire. Similarly with the dog. If one is going game hawking on large tracts of heather moorland an 'English' pointer or one of the setters (preferably an English setter on account of its mainly white coat) would still be the first choice. If one was partridge hawking over the vast root and cereal fields and the setaside of the Fens or East

Anglia a 'bird dog' would still be the favourite but one might opt for one of the larger HPRs such as a GSP or vizsla instead. If one was flying a Harris' hawk or a redtail in small fields, bits of rough and woodland any of the HPRs would suit well (although I expect my own 'English' pointers to cope with brambles in woodland when on the 'pheasant job' which they do extremely effectively) but an austringer flying a gos might favour an English springer or a cocker spaniel although an HPR would do equally well. Were he lucky enough to fly both longwings and shortwings it would almost have to be an HPR since they will invariably work close in cover but 'get out' in the open. So one way and the other there is a large choice of dog for every type of hawking within those parameters.

When I started hawking in the 1950s I flew my female gos over an English springer (the pup and the eyas both cost £8!) and, probably because there was never the end product of the retrieve, she was a remarkably steady little bitch. In my naivety I assumed that *all* gundogs were steady – until I went shooting! I know that many falconers regard a dog as a necessary evil to get slips for their hawk but, fortunately, they also realise that nothing succeeds like success and the more slips they get, the better the hawk will get in terms of fitness, 'the killer instinct' and footing ability. Most falconers acquire a dog because they have hawked with a chum who has one and are then suitably impressed with the amount of quarry the dog finds. Every generation of falconers throws up the dogless 'experts' who search with binoculars for 9 in. grouse in 18 in. heather but most of them eventually either get a dog or give up falconry!

When introducing your dog to hawks (or should it be *vice versa*?) always assume that the worst will happen and you will usually be pleasantly surprised. If you have, say, sparrow hawks or merlins take the pup towards them on a lead with a rolled up newspaper. When the pup is just beyond leash length tap it sharply on the nose with the newspaper and a gruff 'NO' and that should be it. The same process goes for introducing a pup to ferrets. If you took a 7-week-old pup up to my female redtail she would merely regard it as lunch! Therefore use some common sense with the larger hawks and wait until the pup is big enough to get away with being footed if need be. Beware the older, possibly 'rescue', dog. This introduction may take days or even weeks. A game hawker once wanted to buy a pointer dog of mine which I was reluctant to sell because he (the pointer!) would kill any game fowl, training pigeon or even swallow on the wing that he could get his teeth into. Anyway we killed a grouse over him with an old falcon and on taking him up to her on a tight lead while she was pluming the grouse I let him sniff it. Quick as a flash she footed his nose and two weeks later I saw him in a vehicle curled up asleep amidst a cadge of falcons! Get your hawk, particularly Harrises and gosses, used to as many different dogs as you can while they are still eyasses. Feeding in the Grass Yard of the local beagle kennels is good manning and when a client asked me to train and keep his Harris' hawk she was only ever fed on the yard among 20 assorted gundogs - but she still barely tolerates black Labradors! To say that your hawk will not fly with a strange dog present is, in my opinion, merely bad manning. One can frequently incorporate the kennel into part of the mews security and the more that each permanently sees of the other, the better. However, never be tempted to leave hawk and dog loose in the same place.

Having taught your dog the DROP, when calling off your hawk in training blow the SIT or DOWN whistle every time she takes off. The hawk taking off eventually becomes a command in itself to DROP (as in Dropping to Shot for a shooting dog). This helps to prevent the annoying, not to say dangerous, habit of the dog trying to beat the hawk to the quarry! For all other early training leave your hawk in the mews or flight because you cannot train a dog with a hawk on your fist. When teaching HEEL remember to walk the dog on the *right* hand side.

Flying shortwings is relatively easy on both the human and canine system. The austringer merely plods along with hawk on fist (or up tree) while working his dog within that imaginary semi-circle already described, having taught Fido to sit sharply on his bum whenever a rabbit or pheasant erupts. End of story. Flying longwings, however, is a different ball game for both man and dog. To get the best out of it you both have to be fit before you start. If you both go up for your annual stint on 'the bonny purple' overweight and pear shaped, by the time the blisters, aches and sore pads are over it will be time to pack up and go home. Get yourself and the dog fit first and the best way is to go grouse counting or, if that is your 'thing', field trialling on grouse before the season starts. Grouse counting is brilliant training for a young dog but, as I said earlier, with the older dogs I carry a .410 and salute the departing coveys or the old devils do not take it very seriously! If game hawking make sure that there are enough dogs to keep swapping them over and to allow for lame dogs, bitches in season etc. It is extremely demanding for dogs even in cool weather let alone in a 'scorcher' and many dogs have died on the hill through being 'run into the ground' by thoughtless owners. Never pass up the opportunity to let them take a drink or even a dip in any water you come across. If, as is often the case, a party of you go up you should *each* have *at least* one dog and preferably more. Do not leave inexperienced youngsters behind but give them their turn. After a certain stage they will learn nothing in kennels but have to be out there learning their trade. They have to pack a lot of experience into two weeks of the year even if you use the mornings to train while the falcons are weathering. However, fly the 'old stagers' over the young dogs and the eyasses over the experienced ones so as not to disappoint young falcons with false points, points on larks etc. Do not be tempted to use a spaniel to flush the covey at 'the moment of truth' since it will make the pointers 'jealous' and consequently unsteady to the point. If properly trained to rode in on command before dropping to flush and being praised for it there should be no problem. Therefore let the pointers do their own flushing but do not be ashamed of letting youngsters trail a line so that you can control the flush and drop if you have the slightest doubts. There is a school of thought that says that game should not be served a second time or it makes the hawk idle on the first stoop if it knows that the game will be easier to catch the second time round. There may well be some truth in this, but many a 'bird dog' would put a spaniel to shame when winkling a grouse out of thick cover once it has put in!

Finally, whatever your hawking, when the hawk has actually killed the quarry found and flushed by the dog, call the dog up and, once you have made in to the hawk, let it see and sniff the dead quarry and on the first few kills for which the dog is responsible, 'mouth' it as well so that the dog can actually see the end product to all its work. Make a big fuss of the dog (which has done most of the work) and make it feel part of the team, that 'three-legged stool.'

An alley way ensures a direct retrieve.

PLATE 15

'Toby', bred by the author, became a well-known specialist on *les bécasses* in France.

The dog should be dropped before taking the shot.

PLATE 16

Take the dummy before the dog shakes itself dry.

19: Introduction to Gunfire

A gunshy gundog is about as much use as teats on a bull. G.W.

You have only one opportunity to get this lesson right and if you blow it you have, at best, a lot of unnecessary hard work ahead and, at worst, a ruined dog so taking a little trouble is well worth it. Gunshyness is hereditary and gunshy bitches should *never* be bred from. Fortunately it is on the decrease but some of the 'finely bred' dogs still suffer from it. Even so, some dogs are born gunshy while others are made gunshy by an accident that may be within or outside the trainer's control. Recently a stalker shot a fox out of the van window, forgetting his pup was in the back and a friend's son shot a pigeon in the garden with dad's pup tagging along behind - same net result. Gun nerviness is a lesser degree of gunshyness that, with tact, can eventually be overcome. Many pups that have led a sheltered life appear to be gunshy on their public *debut* but are, in fact 'crowdshy' although they *appear* to be gunshy. I fear that we professionals are frequently the worst offenders here! (A GWP bitch of mine that had had some 60 deer shot literally over her bolted for the van on her first pheasant drive. Fortunately she is fine now.) Because your youngster is frightened of thunder, low flying aircraft, etc. does *not* mean that it will necessarily be gunshy. Accustoming baby puppies from Week 1 to banging feed bowls, clapping hands at feed time and thereon throughout their young lives all helps but I had to desist with a litter of very nervous 3-4 week-old spaniel pups as it was making them worse. Nowadays I fire a twelve bore beside the kennels every evening just as I put the training dogs and 'senior puppies' on to feed. Playing around with the pup a long way behind a clay pigeon shoot and then gradually getting closer is all good stuff. One should carry an empty shotgun from time to time during training and swing at imaginary targets.

Always assume that every dog is potentially gunshy. The optimum conditions for teaching introduction to gunfire are a wet, windy day (not uncommon in Mid Wales!) in a large flat open space without a background of hills, trees, buildings or anything to echo the sound. *Avoid* frosty or misty conditions. The ideal weapon is a .410 shotgun followed by a starting pistol held behind one's back and the worst is a dummy launcher. If using a starting pistol hold up a rifle or shotgun in the other hand so that the dog has something with which to identify the noise. Wait until the pupil is at least 9 months old and therefore mature enough to take it and if it has a *familiar* companion for reassurance, so much the better. Send your assistant at least 150 yards *downwind* while you play around with the pup, throwing a tennis ball or whatever. Raise your hand and the assistant fires *immediately* (the timing is crucial) and then walks slowly towards you. Every 20-25 yards you raise your hand and your assistant fires in the air. As long as all is going well he or often she gets closer and closer until only a few yards away. Repeat the exercise with a 12-bore on the next suitable opportunity which also covers introduction to deer rifles. The idea is not to subject the pup to the sound but to amuse it while the sound is merely incidental in the background. The person training on his own will have to sit the pupil, back away for a considerable distance, fire and immediately call the dog in to him (and subsequently watch out for the dog running in to shot). If, however, the pupil slinks in to heel or puts its tail and ears down or looks in the least unhappy back the assistant off some 50 yards (metres) and fire once more. Do not believe that by continuing to fire the dog will get used to it. It will *make it worse*. At least by using this method you can detect that something is amiss before any damage is done.

If you have a dog with a problem there are several ways to overcome it although it sometimes means creating a lesser fault to overcome a major one. I frequently take a nervy youngster beating or picking up on a 300+ bird day when there is a lot of noise but a lot of game/game scent to counter it. (A 30 bird day would only make it worse.) Beating on driven grouse days when the butts are a long way off, letting it chase rabbits in a rabbit infested area and shooting them with a .410 or feeding tripe with the main meal every evening for a week and then having one's faithful assistant firing a shot from a long way off as one puts the food down and getting closer over successive evenings. (This last method can be done on the training ground if you live in a built up area.)

However on 19 out of 20 occasions all will go well and you will wonder why you took all those precautions while the clown who fired a twelve bore over a 7-week-old puppy 'to see if it was gunshy' might wish he had done things otherwise!

20: Out In Anger (at last!)

The best way to ruin a good gundog is to take it shooting. -G. W.

Training does not stop one day and 'proper work' start the next. It is a gradual transition with the dog being trained throughout its first season's shooting or hawking, well into its second and thereafter for the rest of its working life. (The worst bad habits are frequently those acquired by those older dogs that already know the score.) Any gundog's first few outings are very much training exercises rather than a day's shooting and should be purely for the dog's benefit rather than for putting game in the bag. This will require a lot of patience and unselfishness from both you and your shooting companions. This is when all your hard work and effort comes to fruition or goes out of the window. The dog's future in the field will be made or broken by these first few outings *so try to get it right*. How can we minimise those almost inevitable bad habits or unfortunate situations that might creep in? On the training field at home there should be minimum distractions and *you* have set everything up and are totally in control. In the shooting field, particularly on a driven or stand-'n-drive shoot, there is a vast array of distractions and you may have very little say in the matter. Some of these distractions are live and dead game, other dogs (not all of which are necessarily immaculate!), people (not all of whom are necessarily immaculate either!), variable scenting conditions, noise, gunfire, unasked for retrieves and the general 'hooroosh' of the shooting field. However with a little organisation you can minimise these pitfalls and never forget that you will have ten or more seasons work out of that dog so why ruin it for the sake of a few half days shooting? If driven shooting is your main sport you would be wise to wait until *after* Christmas before entering your novice. Things will have quietened down and there will be less 'hype', there will be fewer birds and they will behave more like wild game, any bad habits will not have had time to become ingrained and you have the summer ahead in which to iron them out and by its second shooting season the dog will know what to expect and will be that much more mature. However, for the lone falconer or Gun or one who shoots with one or two chums (for whom most of this book is written) it will be much easier to reduce potential problems. Take the dog out where you expect just enough game for the occasional shot or flight. Make sure that yours is the only dog out - it will do its best to eventually learn enough bad habits on its own without being taught them by some hardened canine criminal! If you already have an older dog work either one or the other but *not both*. The exception to this is when entering any pointing dog when a placid old retriever walking at heel should be used to actually retrieve the game after the pointer has pointed and flushed it. Although you carry a gun yourself let someone else do the shooting so that you can concentrate on the dog. Only take your novice out initially under good or at least fair scenting conditions. Leave garrulous guns at home since shouting upsets sensitive youngsters who think they are being 'rollicked' (particularly true in the beating line on driven shoots) and do not keep the youngster out for too long since, like children, they get tired easily - a couple of hours is plenty. If things are not going too well (Murphy and his mate Sod will soon see to that!) put it on a lead and gracefully retire for the day. Pushing on 'rewardless' can only do harm.

Arrive in good time so you are not 'in a bad hurry.' (I am known in local shooting circles as 'The Late Mr Wallace'!) Leave the dog in the car while you socialise and get your kit sorted out. When all is ready let it out and you can then give it your full attention. Let it 'empty' and then keep it to heel (on the lead if necessary) until you want it to operate. Many young dogs out in company for the first time will play the fool and show off to the gallery. If several of you are out all dressed in 'Barb'r 'n' wellies' you will all look the same to shortsighted youngsters and only when they scent you will they recognise the boss. Most young hunting dogs worth their salt will spend the first twenty minutes or so getting rid of surplus energy after which they drop a gear and settle down. Allow them to do this on game free ground because they are invariably 'too fast for their noses' and will probably try to chase any game they 'bump' to boot. (If you have a young pup with the annoying habit of chasing anything that flies, take it while in training to a field over which swallows are skimming or lapwings wheeling and let it chase them until it is sick of it.) For every yard you walk the dog has to run anything from 40 to 400 yards (metres) on either side so advance at a sensible pace or it will miss out 50% of its ground and therefore 50% of its game (see Fig. 5 on page 72). A 'good going' dog can unwittingly cause you to do this almost without realising it.

When a hunting dog was in training the distance it quartered either side of the handler was strictly adhered to according to the predetermined semi-circle. Now in the field 'in anger', this distance becomes a lot more flexible depending on both the scenting conditions and the amount of game present. In any given situation there is always a point beyond which the dog is simply out of control. The key is always to balance enthusiasm with control and never to let it hunt any further from you than you can easily control. Err on the side of caution. Although I firmly believe that a youngster should *enjoy* itself on its first few outings this should be tempered with common sense. So, without being too much of a martinet, should it 'get carried away' do not allow this to go unchecked. As always, any fault or potential fault should be nipped in the bud before it becomes ingrained and a lot of potential problems can be thwarted by anticipating them and by never taking yours eyes off the dog. If you run a pointing dog in cover higher than the dog, put a dog bell on its collar so at least you know what it is up to. Keep your whistle signals to a minimum and your voice to even less. A noisy handler is always a bad handler and human noise disturbs game. Remember that 'He who hunts best, hunts alone.'

When your pointing dog eventually comes on point leave it on point for a reasonable time and then slowly walk over to one side of the dog quietly reassuring it. As you approach crouch down since a human approaching game will often flush it prematurely. Have your whistle ready and, if necessary, pick up the trailing line. Rode the dog in on command and when the game flushes quietly drop the dog while a Gun hopefully shoots the quarry. Leave the dog on the drop and ask the Gun to pick it by hand. At this stage you do not want your pointer, if an HPR, to associate the flush with a retrieve. If the dead quarry cannot be picked by hand take the dog off at right angles to the line of the quarry's flight and leave the aforementioned 'placid old retriever' to finish the job. *Never shoot game over a pointer that has not first pointed it and then flushed it on command.* Failure to observe this basic tenet will ensure that you end up with a long range spaniel for life!

If you are hunting a spaniel on its first outings keep it well within bounds and as soon as it flushes quarry DROP it. The gun will hopefully shoot the quarry when you or he can again pick it by hand while leaving the dog on the drop. Always hunt any dog on again in a different direction from that just taken by the quarry which avoids an invitation to chase after it. Obviously, most of this chapter also applies to falconry.

If you have a retriever out for its first outing sit it well back behind the Gun(s) so it can see what is going on. Do *not* have it on a lead or it will always expect to be on one. When the first few head of game are shot wait for a few minutes and, leaving the dog on the drop, walk over and pick the game by hand.

Whether HPR, spaniel or retriever, on the way back to the car you may send it for one retrieve into the wind on the quarry that was shot earlier on if not too gory. Pointers, setters and hawking dogs should be shown the end product at close quarters and allowed to smell and 'mouth' it. After one or two outings retrieving dogs may eventually be sent to retrieve the occasional stone dead quarry (verified first by you – 'stone dead birds' have a habit of developing extremely active legs – a few minutes after the shot). One is doing ones utmost to avoid associating the shot with an instant invitation to retrieve. If the dog is somewhat mystified because the dead game does *not* have human hand scent on it rub your hands on the quarry and throw it like cold game. Most dogs quickly get the message. It pays to have a few lengths of nylon tights in your pocket 'just in case'. Corvids, ducks and woodcock are the usual aversions. Up until now all the various lessons have deliberately been isolated instances in the dog's mind. It is only now that we put them all together in the correct sequence that the penny should drop and the pupil realises what we have been banging on about for the last six months!

If you have done your homework all should go reasonably well but you will inevitably have the odd hiccup. Use your commonsense and obey gut feelings – you will have plenty of 'expert advice' from all and sundry! Do not judge the dog's first outing on what it *does* but mainly on what it does *not* do and do not expect too much or you will be disappointed. They all have a lot to learn and it only comes from getting the correct experience over a considerable period of time. Always bear in mind that these first few outings are just the start of a ten or twelve season partnership.

I have included a few 'Do's and Don'ts' from the instructions I give to the owner of every dog I train here (which will already have had game shot over it) below:

On a Driven Shoot including wildfowling/pigeons	*Rough shooting or hawking*
2 half days are better than one whole day	2 half days are better than a whole day
Do not carry a gun yourself	Do not shoot/fly the hawk yourself
Never send the dog straight in to retrieve	Never send the dog straight in to retrieve
Never let it pick dead birds around you	Never let it pick dead birds in the open
Never put it on a runner still in view	Never put it on a runner still in view
Never hunt the dog for first two seasons	Always drop the dog on flushing game in hunting a spaniel

In each case never be afraid to put the dog back on the lead or back in the vehicle.

Although most tyros, quite understandably, view their first outing in public with no little trepidation, if they have done their homework soundly on the right material, they are usually very pleasantly surprised. But do not relax! It is frequently not until the third or fourth outing when young Fido starts to think that he now knows more about the job than you do and you will then have to remind him of his p's and q's. By and large, though, it is a fairly painless operation.

21: This and That

PUNISHMENT

Attitudes have changed radically from a century ago when the Squire's shooting guests, assembled outside The Hall, were addressed thus: 'If the gentlemen would be so kind as to thrash their spaniels we may then proceed with the day's sport.' In today's softer times we read in the 'agony columns' to 'Pet Psychologists': *Q*. 'My rottweiler bites me. What should I do?' *A*. 'Give it a chocolate drop to show you are its friend.'! The answer, of course, lies in the middle.

Punishment of any kind is always the last resort and 'the carrot in front always works better than the stick behind'. Most gundogs are bred to work to please their owners and praise works wonders even on the 'lager louts' (although one sometimes has to look hard for something for which to praise them!). Punishment is not so much about physically hurting the dog but about making it realise it is never outside the long arm of the law. No dog should *ever* be allowed to get away with *anything* because once it has learned that it can you are on the slippery slope downhill. Although a dog can run much faster than we can, the wise trainer always puts himself where he or she can win the battle by using enclosed spaces, corridors, alleys, sloping ground, etc., and correspondingly never giving a command that cannot be enforced. Equally the punishment should fit the crime and there is obviously a vast difference between a pup creeping forward while on the Drop and a young dog doing its utmost to kill a sheep. Punishment can vary from a stern growl to being shaken by the jowls and glared at (which is as much as nine out of ten dogs ever need if done properly) to a couple of sharp cuts with a folded slip lead through to what I once heard described as 'A brief glimpse of Hell'. My dogs all seem terrified of being hit with my tweed cap! It is not only what you do but how, when and where you do it. Again, dogs are extremely territorial by nature and awareness of 'place' is very strong. I can do no better than quote from the late Peter Moxon's excellent book, *Gundogs: Training and Field Trials*, 'Punishment given must be administered immediately the offence is committed and on the exact spot where the pupil did wrong.' It is obviously essential that the dog knows *why* it is being punished and therefore, as always, the trainer must put himself in the dog's position and see the situation from the dog's point of view.

Probably the most frequent question I am asked is, 'What are my views on electric collars?' Having no experience of them myself I am probably not qualified to answer! I suspect that those keenest to use them are the least qualified to do so because they have not trained the dog in the first place and that collars would ruin many more dogs than they made. In America they have 'developed' complete lines of gundog that can *only* be trained with an electric collar which, to my mind, is an appalling state of affairs. Our British gundogs are fortunately, on the whole, much more sensitive and 'trainable'. However, I have come across situations when I could have done with one myself! Last season I picked up with a dominant Labrador bitch that developed the habit of 'mugging' the two younger ones for their retrieves at some distance from me and when yet another blue hare erupts in front of a young pointer three hundred yards above me on a steep Inverness-shire 'face' I would commit murder for one!

I have no quarrel with the *modern* anti-bark collars, though. In this case it is up to the dog whether it chooses to bark or not, knowing full well the consequences. The use of this type of collar, in my opinion, outweighs the prospect of getting rid of an otherwise good gundog just because it is upsetting the neighbours when you are away from home.

However, all punishment can backfire and I often tell the story of a friend house training a monkey in West Africa. Every time it messed on the floor he would smack its backside and chuck it out of the window. After two weeks of this it would mess on the floor, smack its own backside and jump out of the window! Anyone reading this book might be forgiven for thinking that poor old Fido is continually 'in for it' whereas, in reality, most gundogs only need one or two 'rollickings' at most throughout their training. Indeed, some trainers with ultra-sensitive dogs advocate merely taking them back to kennels as a punishment but I, personally, have never tried that one.

When the aggro starts to outweigh the enjoyment it is time to do something about it and if you have a real disaster that makes your life and everybody else's a misery why put up with it for the next ten years. Either re-route it to do a different job elsewhere or have it put down depending on the reason for the aggro. Putting a dog down is *not* cruel to the dog, only possibly to the owner – the dog merely ceases to exist which has to be preferable to the fast lane of the motorway or a vivisection laboratory. If it has nasty social habits like biting people why should you duck your responsibilities and pass your social disaster on to someone else. However, a retrieverholic thug usually makes a good drug-sniffing dog, an unsteady peg dog may suit a picker up or roughshooter, a hard-mouthed dog or sheep killer will often make a good deer dog or a gunshy pointer may well suit a falconer

REPLACEMENTS

It is an unpalatable fact of life that we live longer than our dogs and, once a working gundog has reached double figures, it is on borrowed time. I have never understood why most gundog owners leave getting their next gundog until their present one is on its zimmer frame. This makes no sense at all. Keeping two dogs is no more difficult than keeping one, a young pup gives the older dog a new lease of life, the presence of the older dog helps with some lessons (as already described) and you can gradually phase out the workload of the older dog as the youngster comes on stream. (With heelwork ensure that the old dog that has always walked right beside your left side does not unwittingly force the youngster into a wrong position.) You are also less prone to continually comparing the two (conveniently forgetting what a right hooligan the 'old boy' was as a youngster!).

With a slow maturing HPR you should be thinking of your next puppy when the present dog is 5 or 6 years old whereas with retrievers 6 or 7 is about right and spaniel replacement should be left no longer than 7 or 8 years old. All this means that you are under no pressure to chuck the pup in at the deep end, you can give both dogs half days when the time comes and when the old dog eventually passes on the wrench is lessened. If you have a male dog that was a success you can always go back to the same breeder who probably still has brood bitches of the same bloodline.

HAVING A DOG PROFESSIONALLY TRAINED

A large dollop of mutual trust is involved on both sides so pick a trainer in whom you have confidence, probably from word of mouth. We trainers all wish you to end up with a dog that suits you, even if only because of maintaining whatever reputation we may have acquired along the way! Also pick a trainer who specialises in your breed of dog – it hardy makes sense to send a Labrador to a cocker trainer or *vice versa*. Before arranging to have a dog professionally trained, find out from the prospective trainer what is involved in terms of time and money among other things and arrange to visit the kennels long before you consider sending the dog. In the case of specialist gundogs make sure that he or she has flown hawks or stalked deer or shot geese as the case may be so they know what is required. (I have heard some weird and wonderful tales of deer dogs being trained on multiple dummy retrieves or quartering through the undergrowth like a spaniel looking for deer to be culled!)

Here follows a plea from *all* of us. Please keep your appointments with us trainers punctually. Being late is bad enough (most people have a mobile phone these days if held up) but being *early is far worse*. We all have plenty to do and work to a tight schedule so, if you are early, please wait at the end of the lane! Thanks!

OBSTACLES

Depending on where you live and shoot your dog will come across a great variety of obstacles to negotiate. The more practice it gets on as many as possible early on, the better equipped it will be to do its job. (In Scotland where the stock fences are usually strands of taught high tensile plain wire my dogs, being used to pig netting in Wales, always jump over them rather than slipping easily through them!) On principle, I never assist any dog to the other side of an obstacle that it is physically capable of negotiating itself but leave them to work it out for themselves. They will soon wait to be assisted if you let them and one comes across too many hernias and slipped discs from people heaving overweight pooches over fences! There are exceptions for old dogs, tired dogs and youngsters under six months old when jumping puts an unnecessary and often harmful strain on their limbs and joints. I teach them the command 'OVER' (which means get to the other side of – by going over, under or through!) on low obstacles in my jumping lane *in both directions* and then gradually increasing the height. It is always infuriating when a young dog has not learned that the bars at the bottom of a gate are much closer together than those higher up so I fix stockwire across the bottom rungs of the gates on my training area.

Two problems commonly arise with obstacles. One is the owner or someone else panicking and shouting at the dog which distracts it, sometimes with disastrous results, and the other is when a dog catches a hind leg between the top two wires of a fence. The trick is to put a thumbstick, branch or even (unloaded!) gun barrels crossways at the back of its mouth like a gag (I learned this the hard way when a foxhound panicked…!) and then haul it back *the way it came* by the scruff of its neck when the leg will 'unwind'. Incidentally, the easiest (and cleanest!) way to lift a dog over a fence is to grab the scruff of the neck in one hand and the loose skin over the quarters with the other and lift.

22: Breeding

Like mother, like daughter. Anon.

I frequently come across kind, intelligent people who love their gundog bitch dearly and then breed from her without as much as looking into the subject at all beforehand. There are a lot of bad reasons for breeding from a bitch and precious few good ones. To my mind the only ethical reason for breeding is to carry on a *good* line and keep a pup for oneself. Anything less must be viewed as a form of Puppy Farming.

A lot of pertinent questions need to be addressed long before embarking on a course which carries a heavy responsibility. Is your bitch actually good enough to breed from or would you do better to buy in a pup of different or 'better' breeding? Being clean in the house and not eating the local children is not sufficient reason for breeding from her! Has she any major faults, i.e., hard mouth, whining, uncontrollable out shooting, gunshy, will not face cover or water etc. Have you had her hips and eyes tested once she is over 12 months old? Has she got 'clear' eyes and good hip scores? (0:0 is perfect while 53:53 is as bad as it gets. A TOTAL score of 12 is the *maximum* for a potential brood bitch and preferably a lot lower.) Is she old enough? No breeder should contemplate mating a bitch before her second birthday for two reasons. Before that age she is not physically mature enough to rear a litter *with no long term effects* and you will not know how good she is in the field. Equally, we have found that five years old is usually the practical maximum age for breeding from a maiden bitch. Is there someone at home who can give the pups four meals a day *every day* from three weeks old onwards? What will you do if you do not sell all of the pups? Ten six week old pups is one thing. Ten six-month-old pups is something else! Will you have back any pup that does not suit its new owner for whatever reason? Have you a separate room or building for the 'nursery'? Can you afford to pay out £500-£1,000 in stud fees and travel to the stud dog sometimes staying over in hotel accommodation if she needs a second service, possible vet's fees if anything goes wrong, puppy food, KC Registration, advertising in local newspapers and the sporting press before a single pup is sold? If you can answer all these questions satisfactorily to yourself, then carry on . . .

When should you mate her? You do not want a presumably good shooting bitch out of commission for three months during the shooting season (the last four weeks of pregnancy, the first six weeks of the pups' lives and at least three weeks to recover condition and 'retract her undercarriage'). Equally, the pups should be the correct age (for their respective breed) to start training at the beginning of the following summer. Do not believe that every bitch religiously comes in season every six months. Some do, some do not.

Arrange your stud dog well in advance. Do not wait, as so often happens, until the bitch has actually come in season. Look at his pedigree with a *knowledgeable* friend. Visually check he is *actually* registered with the Kennel Club (often a source of conflict, 'The breeder said he could be registered' etc.). See his hips and eye certificates. Write to the Kennel Club at 1 Clarges Street, Piccadilly, London W1Y 8AB for a Breeder's Form 1 which you take with you to the stud dog. The KC paperwork is seldom return of post even nowadays. Discuss the price of the stud fee with the owner of the stud dog (this is usually approaching the price of a puppy) or whether they wants a pup instead, what happens if the bitch only has one bitch or dog puppy, what happens if she does not 'take' and all the other eventualities. These need writing down at the time (people have short memories!) and should all be discussed *before* the mating.

When you see the bitch 'coming on' apply 'the smear test' by daily wiping a white tissue on her vulva. When she 'shows colour' calculate from there and forewarn the stud dog owner. *Most* bitches 'stand' on the 11th – 13th day. The complete heat normally lasts for 21 days. However, I have known them to only 'take' as early as the sixth day or as late as the eighteenth day. Nothing in 'the plumbing department' is ever certain! However, the best judge are the dogs themselves. From the ninth/tenth day take a male dog of any breed to her daily *on a lead*. She will eventually 'stand' with her tail characteristically cocked over her back and her rear end thrust out. Remove the aforementioned male dog smartly! The *following* day take her to the stud dog. I always arrange to take her back again 48 hours after the first mating as an insurance.

Assuming that she is 'covered' you should assume she is in whelp. Continue to keep her 'in purdah' to prevent another local canine Romeo giving her a 'split litter'. When her heat is finished (and although she may *physically* have finished after the 21 days, she has not necessarily *mentally/hormonally* finished) you may continue to work her as normal for the following four weeks. Once her 'bottom line' [the horizontal line along the bottom of her rib cage extending rearwards along the bottom line of her gut] becomes obvious, ease up on the work. Do not bother to have her 'scanned' by the vet. Either she is in whelp or she is not! (The process is also extremely inaccurate about the actual number of pups since the scan is only two-dimensional.) Keep her relatively active and feed her twice a day but *do not let her get too fat.* She will need to be in her eventual whelping quarters a good two weeks before she is due to whelp. The gestation period is *c* 63 days but a maiden bitch will often whelp up to five days early. The bitch should be dosed for roundworms six weeks (42 days) after mating.

The whelping quarters should fulfil several requirements. They should be damp and draught free *at puppy level.* They should be private. All bitches in the wild are terrified that another dog or a predator will eat her puppies and this fear still persists. They are happiest on their own in the dark. Our current terrier was born down a rabbit hole! The last thing a maiden bitch wants is to put on a 'floor show' under the floodlights in the kitchen with the whole family 'Ooh-ing and Aah-ing'. The whelping quarters should be connected to electricity for a light bulb and, if necessary, an infra red lamp *via* an extension cable if needs be. It should be free of junk or the junk should be boarded off to prevent tiny puppies getting cold, lost or injured. Given the choice, the bitch might just decide that among the garden and workshop tools or behind the freezer is a better place than your lovingly prepared whelping bed.

The whelping bed itself should be raised just off the floor on battens, be large enough for the bitch to stretch out full length, have high enough sides to prevent pups going overboard during the first few weeks and with 'farrowing rails' or some 'give' in the sides. Four wheat straw bales that cannot topple over forming a square on an old door and filled with at least 9 in. (23 cm) of dust-free shredded paper (as sold for horse bedding) works well enough and can eventually all be burned. If the pups are continually whimpering they are almost certainly too cold (or possibly hungry). An agricultural infra red lamp will not set fire to the bed if there is no physical contact. If the pups are all whingeing in a huddled heap the lamp is too high and if all round the sides it is too low. One is trying to achieve the bull's eye effect with a small ring of pups round a 9-12 in. (23-30 cm) blank circle that is directly under the lamp.

When the time comes the average fit, healthy gundog bitch is best left to get on with it with the minimum disturbance, consisting of the occasional quick peek. Always talk to her on your approach since they appear almost deaf at whelping time and should not be startled. Do not handle the pups to 'check' them: you cannot influence whether they are male or female, dead or alive. Above all, avoid the utterly ridiculous practice of taking them away, drying them and weighing them. It only upsets the bitch who wants to lick them dry, thus bonding with them and they weigh whatever they weigh. If everybody keeps coming to look she will try to protect them and end up squashing them. (We keep the family away for four days and strangers away for ten days.) Should you have a dead pup do not remove it in the bitch's presence but wait until she is away from them or she will go looking for it while neglecting the live pups. Should she be straining for more than a couple of hours without producing any puppies it is wise to call the vet but do not be in too much of a hurry to interfere. She will eat the protein rich 'cleansing' so you will not know when she has finished. Keep a close eye on her general behaviour for 72 hours since they very occasionally retain a dead puppy in the womb which decays quickly and is extremely dangerous. When she appears to have finished take her out for a quick walk (you may need a lead) to 'empty' and they appreciate a lukewarm drink of milky, very sweet tea. Then leave her in peace to look after her pups. She may not want to eat for several days after giving birth and so needs tempting with something appetising. They often have a light brown discharge from the vulva for up to a fortnight afterwards.

I have set out a timetable that *we* use here when rearing a litter which seems to work and may act as a guide to anyone who has not reared a litter of pups before:

From Whelping Day

W+ 4 Have tails docked (where applicable), remove dewclaws *especially* any rear ones and cull any deformed/unwanted puppies (a sharp tap on the head).

W+10 Remove the tiny pointed hooks on the puppies' front claws with nail clippers (they scratch the bitch's udder.) For these early 'operations' remove the bitch.

W+14 Register pups with the Kennel Club using Breeding Form 1.

W+20 Remove the tiny pointed hooks on the puppies' front claws again.

W+21 Dose bitch and puppies for roundworm. (Do not be surprised when they produce relatively vast quantities of roundworms - they invariably do!)

W+22 Start feeding puppies with small amounts of food - complete puppy food initially mixed with milk *or* minced tripe/beef and milk on alternate feeds. Lamb milk for bottle fed lambs from your farm co-op at a slightly more diluted rate is better than cows' or calf milk substitute. Initially they will paddle in it, mess in it and generally do every thing but consume it but large (numerically) litters will feed seriously rather earlier then small litters. You will have to keep putting puppies back that waddle off and forget back to feed. After a few days you will get killed in the rush! (Much later on you may have to 'draw' them and hold back the larger more boisterous pups until the smaller ones have fed.) Four meals a day spaced out as far as conveniently possible (07.00, 12.30, 18.00 and 23.00 hrs) works well. Increase amount as pups grow. Start gradually raising height of infra red lamp.

W+28 Introduce an 18% protein adult dog food fed *ad lib* on a permanent (sic) basis in addition to four meals a day.

W+30 Remove hooks from front claws again.

W+35 Advertise puppies in weekly National sporting press. (Monthly magazines earlier.)

W+35 Remove bitch during the daytime for increasing periods over the following week.

W+35 Dose pups for roundworm.

W +42 Advertise in local press for two weeks. Wean pups permanently from bitch and physically keep her away from them(she will be glad of the break!).

W+49 Dose bitch and pups for roundworm. Keep the puppy quarters and its surroundings clean and tidy (first impressions count apart from hygiene) and stand by for potential purchasers. Keep your own chosen pup out of their sight - they always want *that* one! If they want you to keep one for them for whatever reason take a £100 deposit from them. (It concentrates their mind.)

Do not be too downhearted if they are not sold straight away - they seldom are.

You will generally sell the bitch pups easily but the males will 'stick' – yet 50% of the gundogs out shooting are male dogs! You just have to keep on advertising them in the local paper, the vets' surgery, the local gunshop etc. etc. while they eat you out of house and home and systematically destroy your precious property. Never be tempted to sell two pups to the same person, however tempting. It is irresponsible and inevitably ends in tears.

Breeding a litter of puppies is an interesting experience carrying a lot of responsibility; it does the younger family members (who invariably want you to keep all of them!) nothing but good and illustrates vividly how little profit is to be made from rearing a litter of pups! It also reiterates Mr Punch's advice on marriage, 'Don't'!

23: Conclusion

The proof of the pudding is in the eating. Anon.

I can do no better, by way of a conclusion, than to restate those words that I penned some years ago in the conclusion of another book on training: 'There never was such a beast as an "instant gundog" of any sort . . . You will have seen that it takes a lot of time and effort on both sides to achieve the goals to which you have been aiming and, as with anything else in life, you get out of it what you put into it. If you skimp on the training you will end up with a "Mickey Mouse" gundog (which is no more than you deserve) but, if you have done your homework thoroughly and your dog was the right (canine) material in the first place, you will eventually end up with a dog of which you can be proud. You will have trod a path together which is not unlike a game of snakes and ladders – great satisfaction at a lesson learned or an obstacle overcome followed by a spell of wondering whether you had ever tried to train the d—mded thing at all! But gradually the partnership will have begun to gel and suddenly Fido is starting to go about his business as though radio controlled. It is a great feeling.'

To reiterate: get a working bred dog of the correct breed for the job(s), make sure that its upbringing is sympathetic and its subsequent basic training is 110% sound. Ensure that its hunting or pointing or retrieving lessons are soundly taught and then slanted towards its *primary* job to which it should be tactfully entered when ready and then kept at that job for a full twelve months before introducing it to any other facets of your sport.

As I said at the beginning of this book, the ability to train a gundog is not a gift bestowed by The Almighty upon a chosen few. Anybody with half an hour a day, a little of that rare commodity called commonsense and the commitment to own a decent working gundog can, given the right raw material in the first place, end up with a dog that is not only a pleasure to own and which will greatly increase the bag and enhance the pleasure of his chosen sport, but is a dog that he or she can be proud of. Even more important is that that dog will also become a very good friend particularly with the more solitary sports such as wildfowling, deerstalking or pigeon shooting. On your return from a foray in the field, having followed the old cavalry maxim of 'Horses first, weapons next, men last,' you can relax by the fire with a large dram in your hand and your dog by your side to relive the highlights of the day . . .